What You Should Know
to Make More Money
from Your Investments

What You Should Know to Make More Money from Your Investments

ROBERT M. SUTTON

AN EXPOSITION-BANNER BOOK

EXPOSITION PRESS HICKSVILLE, NEW YORK

FIRST EDITION

Library of Congress
Catalog Card Number: 78-72908

ISBN 0-682-49206-X

Printed in the United States of America

CONTENTS

PREFACE

This is not a primer of "How to do it" or a text on security analysis or portfolio management. Knowledge of both of these disciplines is necessary to operate successfully in markets. However, even with such knowledge, my personal observation is that people are not successful investors. Worse yet, neither are most professional money managers, despite their impressive education, work credentials, and access to information. Why is this? There is obviously no one single answer, and much research is being conducted on this very subject. Moreover, it is my strong belief that most investors lack a strong sense of values. They lack clearly defined goals and objectives. And moreover, they lack confidence in their own convictions. This above all else is a necessary first ingredient for successful investing. This book is designed to be a first step in the learning process for the novice to help himself develop the necessary psychological and fundamental framework for better investing.

Preface

I would like to express my thanks to my editor Linda Popofsky, to Professor Stan Fish for his counsel, and to my wife and children for the sacrifice they have endured while this book was incubating. I would also like to acknowledge the cooperation and use of data and charts from the Cleveland Trust Company, Securities Research Company, Philip E. Chew of Josephthal & Co., Ned Davis of J. C. Bradford & Co., Henry Blackstock of Wertheim & Co., and David L. Babson & Co., Inc.

What You Should Know
to Make More Money
from Your Investments

I

SET YOUR OBJECTIVES

Making money in the stock market seems a simple enough affair. It certainly is the topic of a lot of conversations. How often have you heard, "What did the market do today?" "Where's the Dow?" "Do you think the market's going up?" When people find out my profession at dinner parties, I'm often cornered for endless hours listening to a litany of successes or failures. Everybody seems to have his own opinion about how to succeed in the market, but I'm convinced very few people are really successful in investing in the market on a consistent basis. Even professional money managers have fared poorly. If we look at the record, during the past ten years, the average institutional portfolio of equities, including reinvested dividends, was up only 2.5%. Were we to investigate the various classes of professional managers—investment counsels, banks, mutual funds—the results would not be much different. Why is this? Simply because the odds of beating the market are stacked against you in the long run. Studies have shown that very few institutional investors have achieved returns in the 8-10% area on a consistent basis during the past ten years. Despite these dismal results, I'm convinced other factors are also at work that have a strong bearing on the odds. After many years in the business, I believe that both the individual investor and the institutional investor can increase their odds of success by following some basic steps. That's what this book is about. You don't need elaborate formulas, computer programs, or higher mathematics. You don't need to be a trained security analyst or portfolio manager. Obviously, knowledge of financial statements is essential. But if you apply some of the basic tenets of this book diligently, you can increase the odds in your favor. This book cannot tell you "how to do it" but it can put you on the road to success in today's market.

The first thing to do is to set your goals. This sounds easy. However, most people do not have a fixed objective in mind. Have you ever sat down and actually written on a piece of paper what you are trying to accomplish with your money? Believe it or not, probably ninety percent of investors don't really care whether they make money or not. I have met many different kinds of investors and classify them into four basic types. All have the same basic characteristic; namely, they are not in the market *really* to make money, but to fulfill other psychological motivations.

The first type can be called "the gambler." This is the person who is in the market for action. His conversation easily identifies his motive. He wants to know "what's moving? what looks good?" It doesn't matter whether it's steel, chemicals, autos—just as long as it's "hot" or in "vogue." One of my closest friends was a gambler par excellence. He never failed to call me every day to find out what was happening and how things looked. Even when traveling in Europe or the Far East, he would make a point to call to check in and go over his list of stocks. This type always craves action—no matter what form. For instance, my friend successfully played the currency game a few years ago when the dollar was weak against the mark and the Swiss franc. The thrill, the excitement, the motion, was the essence of investing for him.

The second type can be called "the country club type." This kind of player doesn't really know why he holds his stocks. But someone once told him that IBM is "like a Picasso" so he bought it and didn't sell. He impresses you with his cost basis. The "country club type" adheres to the old standards—the companies that were great investments twenty or thirty years ago. Many may be even lucky enough to hold some of the newer favorites of ten years ago—like Xerox or Polaroid—because an investment counselor tried to spice up their portfolios. What is frustrating about many of the country club set—or "little old lady" types—is that they usually turn out to be the most successful investors over time, despite a lack of insight. A number of years ago, when reviewing a portfolio of an elderly lady, I was highly impressed with the quality of her list of holdings and their original purchase prices. I couldn't help but ask her how she could have been so astute and successful these many years. She simply smiled, saying that she really didn't know too much about stocks, but that since she knew that generals were the highest ranking officers in the Army, she was certain she couldn't go wrong buying General Motors, General Electric, General Telephone, General Foods, and others. She had made most of her purchases in the 1930s. How staggering and humbling a response!

The third player is the "macho" type. He must be a winner. He's in the game to prove he's better than anyone else. His conversation reveals him—he always wants to know how you did last quarter, last year, and how you're doing this year. He wants to know your favorite stock so he can match it with his current choice. (Frankly, it is none of his business.) He's always quick to let you know how well he's doing, and how much money he made on his last winner. (He never tells you about his losers.) He claims he never makes a mistake and chalks his losers up to someone else's stupidity. This guy is the worst type. He makes you feel inadequate and stupid. Why weren't you up 50% last year, or 20% in the first quarter? Why didn't you own Levitz or Payless Cashways or MGIC when they were soaring? Didn't everybody? Usually these players operate by their own rules and the investment scoreboard is littered with their wrecked hopes and desires.

The last type is the opposite of the "macho" player—"the masochist." He never wins! No matter what he does, it's wrong. He usually buys on top of a move and sells in frustration at the bottom. He lacks confidence in his own opinions and consistently follows the crowd. He's constantly reading broker's reports. It doesn't matter that the story may already be discounted, just so long as it seems reasonable and the stock is "acting" okay. (What this means I really don't know, but everybody uses the term in the investment business. I suppose it means the stock is going up before it goes down!) Soon after he buys XYZ because it's "acting okay" and everybody is talking about it, some negative news gets printed in the *Wall Street Journal* and a wave of selling engulfs our hero. He quickly calls his broker for the latest interpretation of the negative news—and is quickly informed, of course, that time is needed to "digest" the news. So our hero sells out, as the "nays" have it for the moment. No sooner does he complete his sale, then he finds that the negative news wasn't really that negative at all. No matter, our hero is off on a new quest.

If you see yourself in any one of these characters, you needn't read on. You are not really interested in making money. Making money is a *serious* business. You must truly *want* to make money. It takes dedication, determination, hard work, study, sacrifice, timing, and luck. Most people are content to compromise their goals and ambitions. What are yours? Write them down on a piece of paper. Don't be afraid to be ambitious. Put it away so you can check your progress.

Having written down your goals, you are now in a position to begin to construct your personal balance sheet. Write down all of your assets—cash in the bank, cash value of insurance, car, home—whatever has a realistic market value. On the right-hand side, list all of your liabilities—installment contracts, mortgage, charge accounts. The difference is your net worth. I think you will find this exercise most revealing. What's more, very few people go through this process. Without it, they cannot know where they're at or where they're going.

This step is also important as you can now relate your assets to your goals in completely dispassionate terms. Have you set down contradictory objectives, or are you creating the impossible goals that can only cause you frustration? That doesn't mean that you should not set high standards for yourself. What's important is that you have to choose your approach with care. Perhaps you'll have to take more risks. For example, let's say you have $10,000 and would like to double your money in five years. That's equivalent to a 15% compounded rate of return, no mean accomplishment by anyone's standard. Moreover, in our example, we have assumed that you would be successful in each and every year. That means you will have to make $1,500 the first year, $1,725 the next, until you doubled your original investment. However, knowing that mistakes will be made—the market could go down instead of up—you ought to allow for some losses. It's not unreasonable to say that after three years you get caught in a bear market and refuse to sell out, losing 25%. What this means is that the next year you have to be up 33% just to be even, and then must compound your return from the bottom at 75% just to reach your original goal of doubling your money in five years.

It doesn't sound as easy as you first thought, does it? Well, it isn't! The higher you set your goals, the greater the risks become. Just be aware of the game you have to play; otherwise, settle for the more modest ambitions. Books abound on every aspect of investing—from real estate to stocks—telling you how to run $10,000 into a million. If the author was so smart he probably wouldn't be writing to tell you his formula. That's simply against human nature! If it were easy to make a million the world would be full of millionaires, and we book writers would have no one to tell how to do it.

In summary, Step One is to set your goals—in writing. Next, you list your assets and liabilities in relation to your objectives. Make sure that they are reasonable and that you can afford to lose. Go ahead and set aggressive objectives, but be aware of the risks you must assume to reach your goals. Finally, review your progress periodically in relation to your objectives for necessary changes and modifications.

II

KNOW THYSELF

This is probably the most important chapter in this book. Although most people do not set out explicit objectives for themselves, often, subconsciously, they know what they're trying to accomplish. However, without "knowing yourself," it is virtually impossible to be a successful investor over any extended period. The reason is straightforward. Without understanding your strengths and weaknesses, you cannot develop a coherent philosophy or disciplined approach to investing. This approach ought not to be someone else's; it should be yours—an approach with which you feel comfortable, which reflects your personality, your way of reaching your goals. Without this self-analysis you will lack direction, discipline, and backbone. Therefore, Step Two is know thyself.

Take that pen in hand again, and list your strengths and weaknesses. What are your characteristics? Do you scare easily? Do you tend to be confident? Overconfident? Unsure of yourself? What are your prejudices? Are you stubborn? Do losses tend to shatter you? Do you have a tendency to try to make killings? Are you emotional? Do you have a cold-blooded approach to problems? Are you analytical or intuitive? What is your breaking point? Be honest! You'll see how important this exercise will be later, particularly when you begin to invest. Frankly, there is no one way to make money, no one successful formula, philosophy, or methodology. But without appreciating your own personal characteristics you can fall prey to the unscrupulous or whimsical.

A few years ago, it was fashionable to believe that one could determine the personality type by the stocks that person held. For instance, someone whose portfolio was predominantly characterized by low price/earnings was considered conservative, unimaginative, dull, insecure. One with high P/Es (growth companies) was considered aggressive, secure, daring, imaginative, and avant-garde. All of this is nonsense for the truly liberated investor, who never worries what others may think of his holdings. He keeps his style flexible to meet changing markets because he is interested in making money. He may have a propensity towards a particular style which maximizes his strength and minimizes his weakness, but he's not a prisoner of his personality. He understands himself completely and has developed a unique style built around a consistent philosophy.

Once you have listed your strengths and weaknesses and taken the time to think about them, list the traits that are essential for successful investing.

The first trait is confidence—confidence in your opinion, confidence in your judgment. Without confidence, you cannot hope to win. You must have that good, inner feeling to be able to withstand pressure, back away from losses cheerfully, and be tenacious when necessary. Confidence also includes self-reliance. An investor must be able to arrive at his own conclusions and not get swept up in the optimism or pessimism of the crowd.

However, the investor should not assume that confidence means arrogance. The graveyard is full of stories of people who thought they were smarter than the market. The greater your exposure to the market the more respect you develop for this incredible discounting mechanism. Confidence also implies humility: there is always someone, somewhere, who knows more than you do, who has more up-to-date information or is aware of an upcoming event to affect your stock's future. I remember the story of a leading photographic analyst who was so bullish on Polaroid in 1972 that he even hinted that arrival of the SX-70 would seriously erode Eastman Kodak's profits and dominance of the industry. At that time Polaroid was selling in the 90s and since there was considerable speculative appeal the stock shot up to the 130s in no time. With the introduction of the camera the price of Polaroid stock seemed to crest and began to fall. Problems with the batteries in the film pack were followed by difficulties with the yields on film production. The price of Polaroid continued to sink, yet this analyst went on publishing bullish reports, dismissing each problem as a minor nuisance. He was certain he was right, despite what the market was saying. Polaroid eventually declined from the 130s to the mid-teens in 1974. So be confident, but not arrogant.

Judgment is the second trait essential for success. Unfortunately it is a trait that cannot be taught, but only acquired from experience. In his classic book, *Battle for Investment Survival*, Gerald L. Loeb observed that his success came not from being more right than anyone else, but from his ability to quickly judge which of his own ideas were incorrect and to take appropriate action. You obviously can acquire through study the skills necessary to make good decisions. But nothing can take the place of actual experience, especially in the market. An excellent way to get that experience is to set aside a small fund for "learning" purposes before beginning a full-scale investment program. In this way you can test "live" all that you've absorbed. You can test your psychological reaction to real events. There is nothing like putting some real money on the line—not a paper portfolio, but real money. Not only will this experience be invaluable to you before you start a full investment program, but it will help build your self-reliance. Confidence is a self-reinforcing process, and good judgment breeds confidence.

A successful investor needs courage—the confidence to act on his own judgment. It's not enough to be right about a stock; you must be both right and have invested in it to profit. Many people who seem to call the market turns with unusual clairvoyance, turn out to have lacked the courage of their convictions and own none of the stock. Buy when your judgment dictates! Courage needs to be coupled with prudence. Aggressiveness and courage are necessary, but in today's market the key is to be discriminatingly bold. Too much courage, coupled with too little prudence, eventually leads to major losses.

Flexibility—the capacity for revision or changing one's mind—is also essential to successful investment. The photography analyst we discussed earlier was not only arrogant, but unable to change his mind until it was clear that he was wrong. He clung to his position despite the market, despite overwhelming evidence to the contrary. Learn when to sell and cut your losses. The ability to admit errors will make you lots of money over time, by cutting short your mistakes and adapting to changing markets. While flexibility is essential, don't change your mind too often or you'll exhaust yourself in the decision-making process. You will have to develop patience. This is one of the most difficult traits to cultivate, particularly when everyone around you seems to be doing better than you. There is nothing worse than looking at the paper on an active day and finding that your stock hasn't moved. It may be an omen, but more than likely buyers and sellers were just evenly matched on that particular day. If you have selected well, and the reasons you bought your stock in the first place are still valid, then sit tight. You just may have been early. It takes confidence in one's own judgment, courage in one's own convictions, and a quiet tenacity to hold on when you know you are right.

The importance of confidence and patience together cannot be overestimated. I remember purchasing Getty Oil in the mid-50s in the summer of 1970. At that time, there were no brokerage reports and few analysts followed the company. However, my analysis suggested that the price of oil in the United States was likely to be under heavy, upward pressure over the next few years. Getty was an unbelievably leveraged way to play this trend since this company had tremendous price leverage from existing production. Getty also had the capacity to expand its volumes to produce double leverage, and, even better, they had the "cash flow" to explore for more oil. The environment for oil stocks was good, and Getty stock moved up to the 90s by the early spring of 1971. At a New York Society of Security Analysts presentation in January of 1972, it was announced that company earnings would be down moderately for the year, as Getty expected to increase its spending on exploration. Trading was immediately halted, and when the stock reopened down sharply, there were nothing but disconsolate faces among the analysts. While I was disappointed that the progression of earnings was going to be interrupted, the reason that I bought the stock was still completely valid. In fact, the increased spending for exploration only tended to confirm my initial analysis that the economics for the oil industry were favorable. Getty stock finally bottomed out in the low to mid-70s during the summer of 1972 and subsequently rose to about 210 in 1976. My judgment had been vindicated—and so had my patience.

One mustn't confuse patience with stubbornness. If the facts are still intact, the story not yet fully discounted, then hold on. But when the facts change, and you insist you are still right, you're being stubborn. Remember our photography analyst; not only was he arrogant and inflexible, but he was stubborn. Don't forget, in the last analysis, the market is always right.

Putting this all together, you will need the *confidence* to make and act upon your own conclusions, *judgment* gleaned from experience, the *courage* of your own convictions, *prudence*, the *flexibility* to change your mind, and, finally, *patience*. All of these characteristics are related. By experimenting with a small amount of money before you launch your investment program, as mentioned earlier, you will be able to find out which of these personal traits are really characteristic of you. Which ones need strengthening? Are your weaknesses what you thought they were? How do you rate when it comes to the six necessary investment traits?

III

DEVELOP AN INVESTMENT METHODOLOGY

Assuming that you have experimented with some real money, you probably have developed a style of your own. You're beginning to think about ways to make profits. But there is no one system, no one way that leads to success in the market. I am constantly amazed how many different ways there are to make money. Recently I was going over the portfolio of a friend who runs a highly regarded hedge fund and was surprised to find no growth stocks to speak of, no cyclicals or energy stocks—yet he was doing far better than the market. He had concentrated his efforts on severely depressed stocks and low P/E stocks of companies with rapidly expanding earnings. What is important, though, was that he was fully conscious of his strategy and could articulate a definite methodology that reflected his own way of doing things.

That's the key! After you set your goals, understand your strengths and weaknesses, and begin to have a sense of style, you should develop a methodology for your investment program. I cannot overemphasize the importance of a methodology. It's the knot that ties everything together. The reason is simple. A methodology provides a systematic and consistent framework to approach problem-solving. In this case, a successful investment program is your goal. This program should reflect your beliefs, your personality. Again, this is best learned from experience and experimentation. It cannot be easily taught. You can benefit from others by reading about their successes and failures. I would suggest the continued use of your experimental fund to sharpen your personal investment philosophy. Write it down on a piece of paper. Obviously, it must be grounded in realistic and fundamental truths. Equally important, if your methodology is systematic and consistent, it will constantly force you to be disciplined in your approach. Those three words say it all—systematic, consistent, and disciplined. If you can master those three attributes, combined with proper goal-setting and knowing yourself, you will be on the road to successful investing.

To provide a head start and whet your appetite for further reading and experimentation, I will describe four broad investment philosophies that are adaptable to most markets.

1. TURN-AROUND COMPANIES

The first philosophy emphasizes turn-around companies—companies which have had poor earnings records and have taken steps to change this situation. There is nothing more exciting and exhilarating than to discover, study, invest, and then see your money multiply when others recognize a changing company. A turn-around can take many forms. It can involve a sale of assets, the redisposition of assets, the dropping of lines of business, the purchase of assets, etc. These moves may be taken by existing management or, more than likely, by new management. Typically, a turn-around situation is a low-profit earner with a spotty record. New management takes steps to improve overall profitability and develop a more consistent record. The successful turn-around can lead to spectacular market profits. General Mills provides us with a classic textbook case. Under the leadership of Charlie Bell and Ed Rawlings, a program that "rationalized" the company was established and a goal of "consistent, above-average growth" was established. During the postwar period, General Mills had diversified into many businesses—appliances, electronics, grain-milling, cereal production, packaged foods. The record was cyclical and undistinguished. The stock made little money for its holders during the period 1945-1957, ranging from a low of $7 a share to a high of $13 a share as indicated on the chart on page 30.

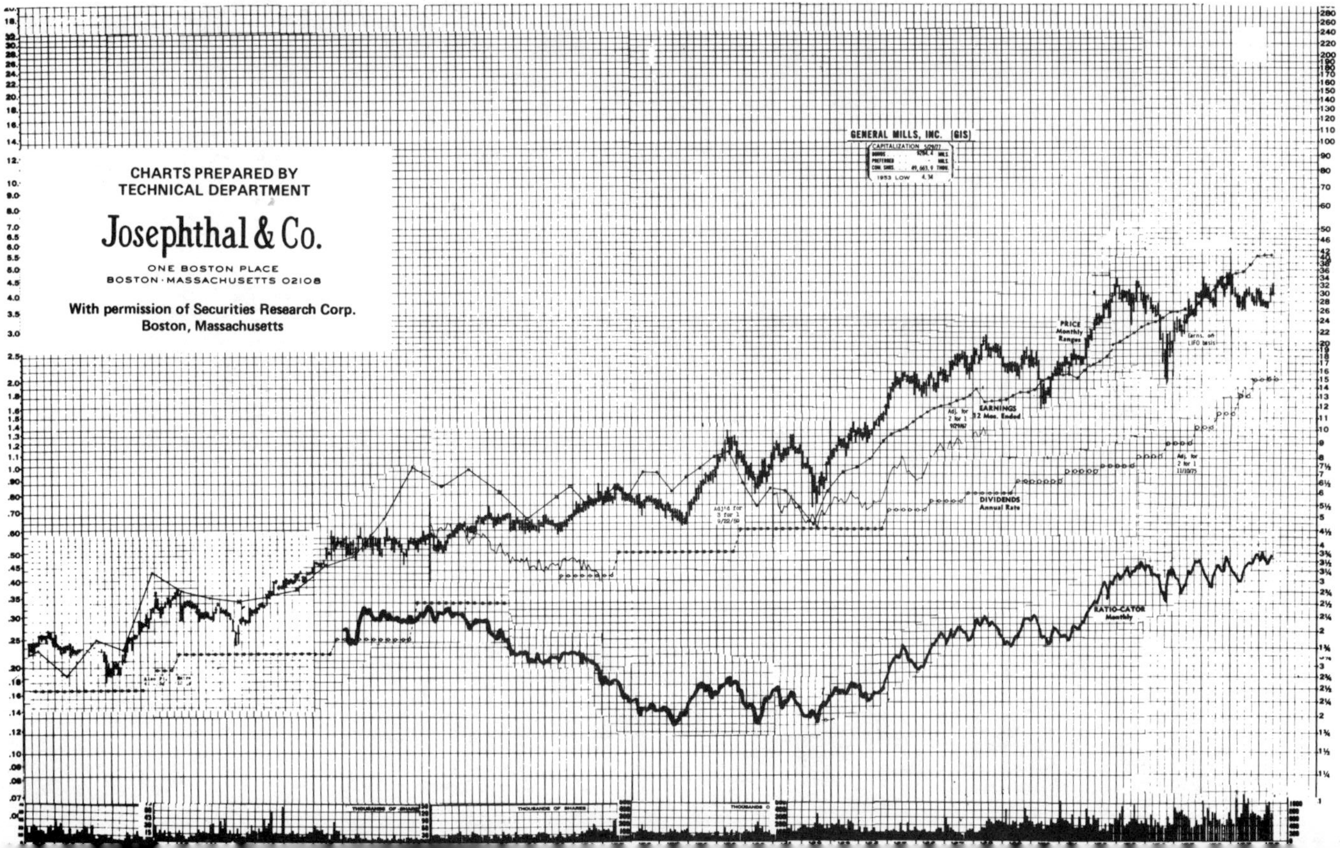

CHARTS PREPARED BY
TECHNICAL DEPARTMENT

Josephthal & Co.

ONE BOSTON PLACE
BOSTON · MASSACHUSETTS 02108

With permission of Securities Research Corp.
Boston, Massachusetts

General Mills' turn-around plan called for the sale of assets where a low rate of return existed, the disposition of businesses in which the company had no expertise, and those businesses which were basically cyclical and capital-intensive. Management concentrated time and assets on the company's strengths in marketing packaged foods. The plan was implemented in 1961-62 and the results were startling. So was the stock's performance.

General Mills' stock appreciated about 166% when the change was fully recognized in the market, and today it is considered a blue-chip holding. Other great turn-around stories include Chrysler in 1962. A clever marketing strategy by new management and a favorable economic environment propelled earnings from $1.74 in 1962 to $5.46 in 1964. The stock price was even more spectacular, rising from 10 in 1962 to a high of 60 in 1964 for a gain of 500% over that time span. Revlon stock appreciated 140% from about $25 to $60 in just eighteen months after management reversed a poorly conceived diversification and acquisition policy and concentrated on their basic business of cosmetics. Still another turn-around situation was Westinghouse which advanced 100% over a twenty-seven month period as the revitalization plan under Don Burham took hold.

While these stories seem to make turn-around investing exciting, there are many pitfalls.

First, it takes considerable knowledge to evaluate management's plans. Second, competition is not likely to remain quiescent. For the investor, considerable patience may be needed, to say nothing about "false starts." Turn-arounds can literally take years to accomplish and the resultant payoff can be disappointing. For example, it took about ten years to make Montgomery Ward a viable competitor in retailing. For their stockholders, the waiting proved unrewarding and frustrating. Mobil Oil, who now controls Montgomery Ward, is likely to gain the fruits of management's labors.

Then again, many turn-arounds do not end up as "true" turn-arounds. General Mills and Revlon are the exceptions. More often than not the company will revert back to its old status—it's just too hard to shake off history and change company characteristics. Chrysler is again a marginal company, and Westinghouse is again in a "turn-around situation." The odds are heavy against the turn-around player—but should he luck out, the profits can be handsome. Remember the risks and that patience is required.

2. CYCLICAL STOCKS

Another popular investing methodology involves the purchase and sale of cyclical stocks. Since the majority of all listed securities are essentially cyclical in one way or another, this is one of the most widely practiced philosophies around. It really boils down to "buying low" and "selling high." Its followers spend a great deal of time studying current and future business prospects for the overall economy. This is important since most cyclical companies' prospects are closely tied to the general economic trend. Cyclical stock investors must necessarily become "armchair" business-cycle economists, and develop a feel for the "economic time clock." Investing can cover a wide spectrum of industries—copper, steel, aluminum, retail trade, finance, machinery, petroleum, chemicals, insurance, and on and on. Many people prefer to concentrate their efforts on a few selected industries, getting to know their companies and businesses better that way.

Cyclical investing can be broken down into three main categories, each with its own characteristics. First is the typical cyclical company. This is a mature company whose earnings are directly tied to the business cycle. Growth is moderate at best and more often earnings have shown very little progress over time, but there are wide swings. The same can be said of stock prices for these companies. Kennecott Copper is a good example of a cyclical company (see chart on page 34). Note the wide swings of earnings and share prices over the years. By attempting to buy low and sell high, the investor hopes to profit by these wide swings.

The next category is cyclical longer-duration. These companies are also mature and sensitive to the general economic trend. However, their cycles can last longer than the first category. Earnings can grow rapidly for an extended period of time. The trend of stock prices can often resemble the trend of growth stock prices when this is happen-

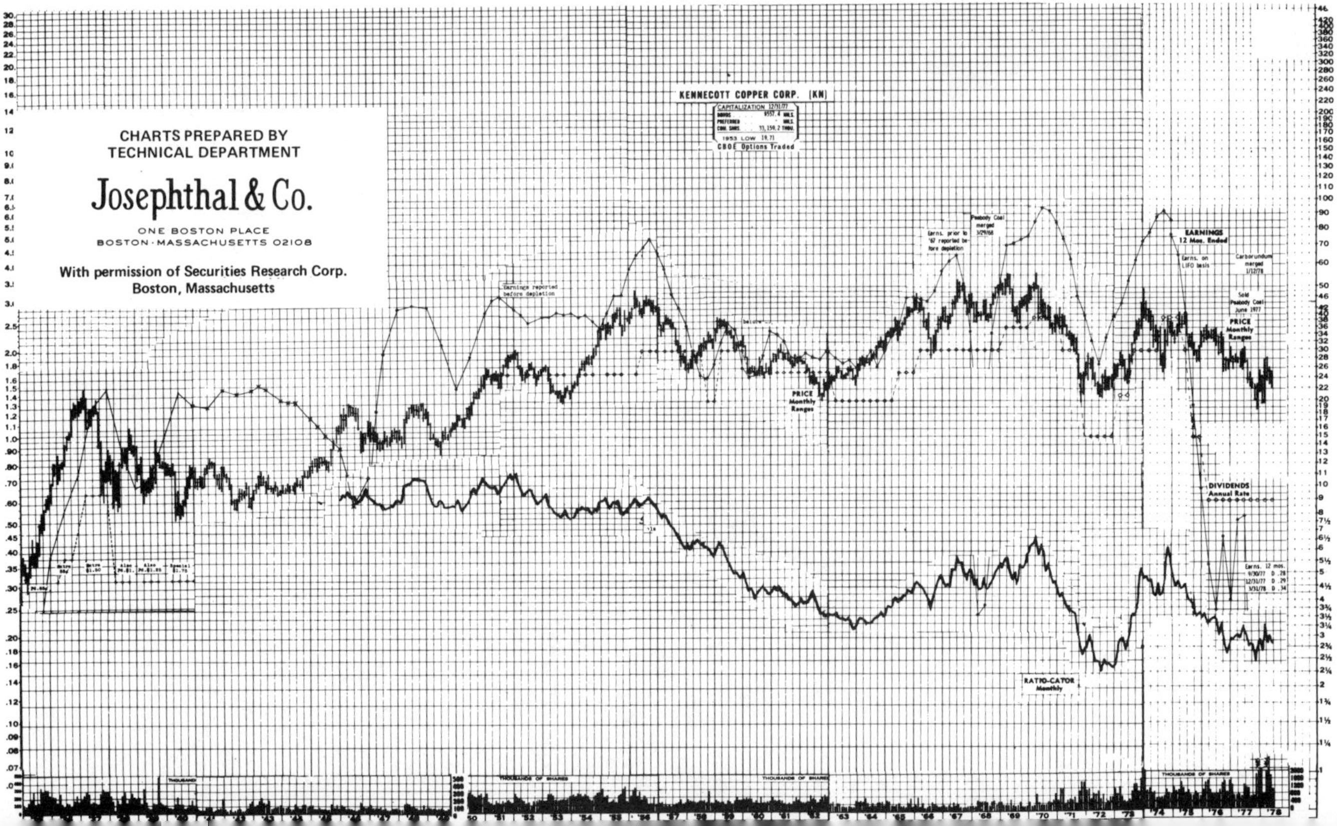
CHARTS PREPARED BY
TECHNICAL DEPARTMENT
Josephthal & Co.
ONE BOSTON PLACE
BOSTON · MASSACHUSETTS 02108
With permission of Securities Research Corp.
Boston, Massachusetts
KENNECOTT COPPER CORP. (KN)
CAPITALIZATION 12/31/77
1953 LOW 19.71
CBOE Options Traded
Earnings reported before depletion
Earns. prior to '67 reported before depletion
Peabody Coal merged 3/29/68
EARNINGS
12 Mos. Ended
Earns. on LIFO basis
Carborundum merged 1/12/78
Sold Peabody Coal June 1977
PRICE
Monthly
Ranges
DIVIDENDS
Annual Rate
Earns. 12 mos.
9/30/77 D .28
12/31/77 D .29
3/31/78 D .34
RATIO-CATOR
Monthly
THOUSANDS OF SHARES

ing. Weyerhaeuser (see chart on page 36) is a good example of a cyclical longer-duration type company. The 1972-1973 period was definitely favorable, and earnings exploded. So did the stock price.

The final category is growth-cyclical. Here, the company is also sensitive to general economic trends, but earnings display some growth characteristics. By that, we mean that each trough or low point in earnings is higher than the previous trough, so that by connecting troughs (or peaks) in earnings one can discern an underlying growth trend. As an illustration, look at the chart of Caterpillar Tractor Company. Share prices have shown wide swings but have generally been upward. The same can be said of earnings as each trough or plateau is higher than the previous one.

Cyclical investing can be fun and exciting. If you can master its techniques, it can be very profitable. However, there are many dangers. First, of course, by definition, you must buy "low" and sell "high" to make money. This is more easily said than done. Timing becomes important and most people are simply not good at "calling" stock turns. Next there are some powerful psychological negatives to overcome. Most often, share price lows and highs do not coincide with "actual" earnings lows and highs, forcing you to discount or anticipate earnings to a greater extent. Now you run the risk of either "selling too soon" or, in your enthusiasm, projecting earnings at an unattainable level. Crowd psychology tends to be strong and

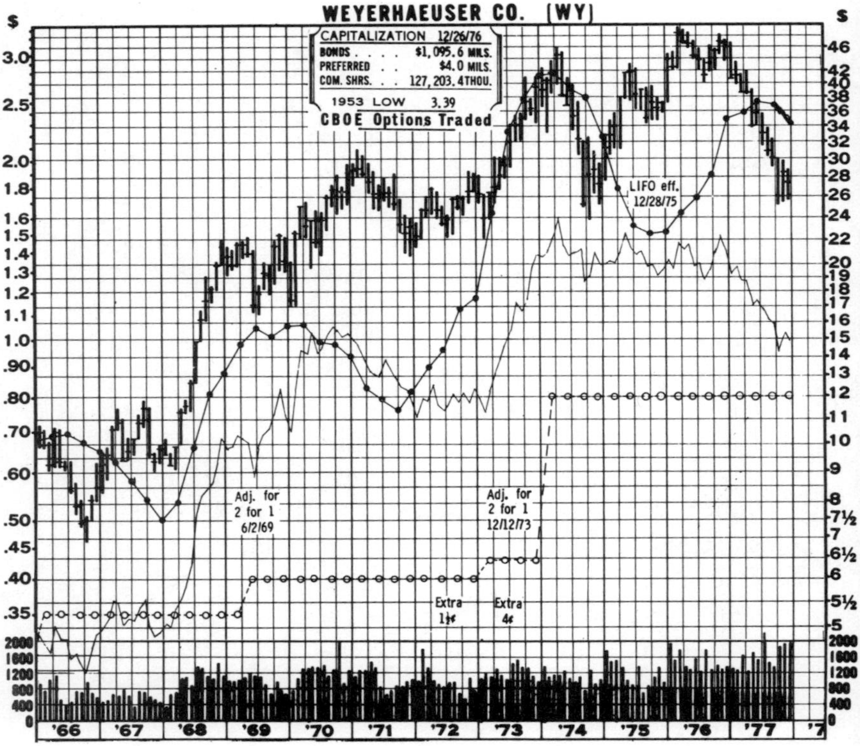

WEYERHAEUSER CO. (WY)
CAPITALIZATION 12/26/76
BONDS . . . . $1,095.6 MILS.
PREFERRED . . $4.0 MILS.
COM. SHRS. . . 127,203.4THOU.
1953 LOW 3.39
CBOE Options Traded
LIFO eff. 12/28/75
Adj. for 2 for 1 6/2/69
Adj. for 2 for 1 12/12/73
Extra 1½¢
Extra 4¢
'66 '67 '68 '69 '70 '71 '72 '73 '74 '75 '76 '77

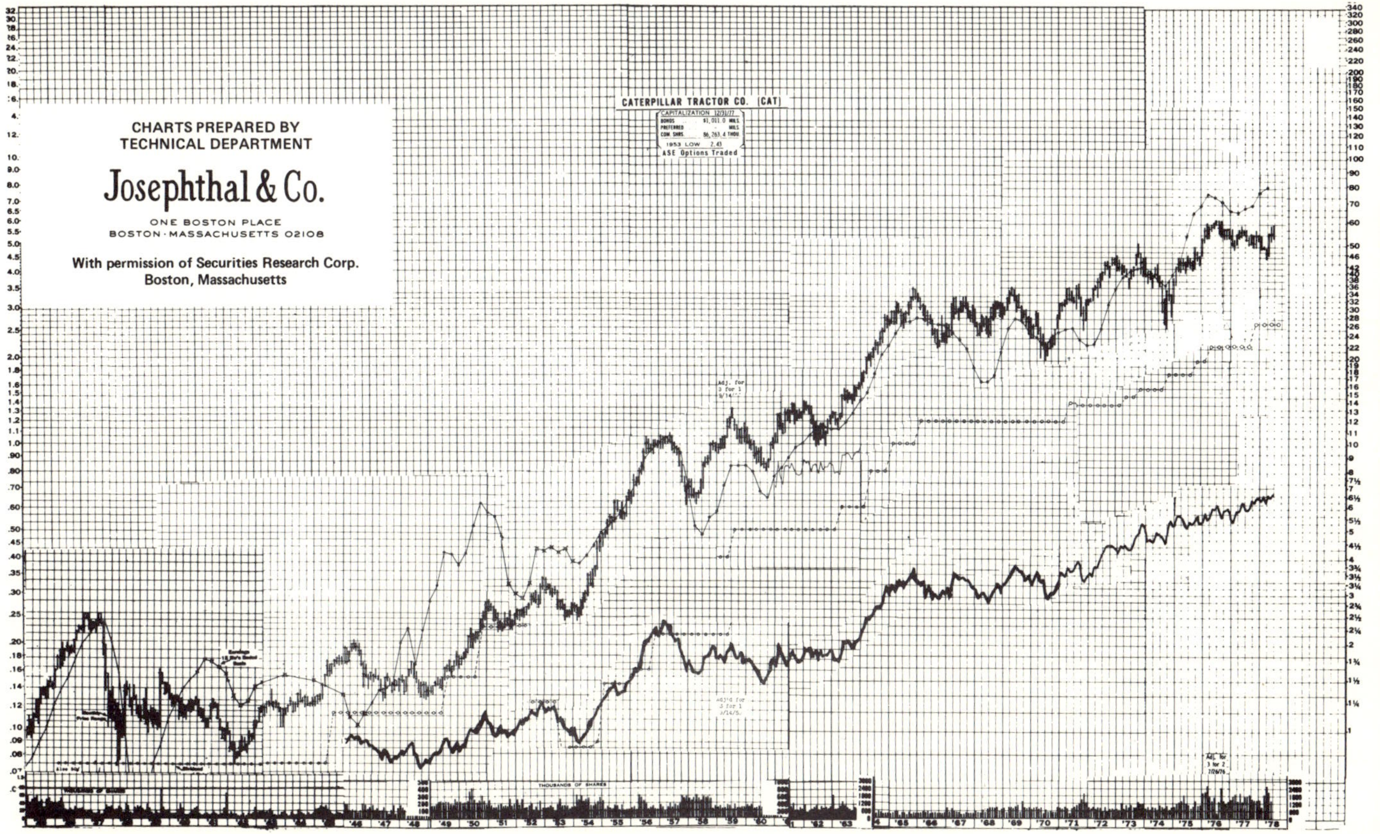
CHARTS PREPARED BY
TECHNICAL DEPARTMENT
Josephthal & Co.
ONE BOSTON PLACE
BOSTON·MASSACHUSETTS 02108
With permission of Securities Research Corp.
Boston, Massachusetts
CATERPILLAR TRACTOR CO. (CAT)
CAPITALIZATION 12/31/77
BONDS $1,011.0 MILS
PREFERRED MILS
COM. SHRS. 86,263.4 THOU
1953 LOW 2.43
ASE Options Traded
Adj. for 3 for 1
Adj. for 3 for 2 7/26/76
THOUSANDS OF SHARES
'46 '47 '48 '49 '50 '51 '52 '53 '54 '55 '56 '57 '58 '59 '60 '62 '63 '65 '66 '67 '68 '69 '70 '71 '72 '73 '74 '75 '76 '77 '78

you must be able to "cross the crowd." Also there can be long time periods between peaks and valleys. As I mentioned earlier, if you can master cyclical investing techniques and have a "thick skin," this type of investing can be very profitable.

3. INCOME AND LOW PRICE/EARNINGS RATIO SECURITIES

A third widely followed investment methodology is concentrating on income and low price/earnings ratio securities. The notion here is that income stocks, because of their relatively high yields, will afford downside protection and will advance in an up market. The same could also be said of low P/E stocks with the added kicker that multiples could expand, thereby giving additional upside leverage.

Income stocks usually represent mature companies with low growth rates. They can cover a broad list of industries. Many cyclical companies are essentially income stocks. Those who follow these companies necessarily have to pay close attention to general economic trends, especially the interest-rate cycle.

For my part, I see little merit in investing primarily for dividends or playing the interest-rate cycle through income stocks. Earnings are a much more important consideration than dividends per se in judging the attractiveness of an individual stock. There are many examples of companies which maintain dividends of a stated amount, but the price of the stock is gradually on the decline. Continental Corp. is a good case in point. Until recently, despite a stable dividend of two dollars a share in the 1965-1972 period and rising dividends each year since 1972, stock market prices were still substantially below the peak achieved in 1965. It is clear that the declining earnings trend overpowered the steady increase in dividends. Obviously, the market questioned the ability of the company to continually raise the dividend while earnings were still in a declining trend.

The important thing to be stressed with regard to dividends is that in themselves they do not matter much. It is *earnings* that really count in making a stock attractive. Buying simply for dividends is a static concept. It is rising earnings and the company's ability to pay "increased" dividends that count. A high dividend yield is generally a warning for the potential investor to look around for the reasons that the stock looks cheap. This does not mean that money cannot be made buying income stocks. You must look primarily to more dynamic factors—such as changing earning power which will lead to increased dividends. Many proponents of income-stock investing place great emphasis on total return, that is, a high dividend and capital appreciation. The greatest part though of the "total return" will be the capital appreciation and *this* is dependent upon the outside factors I mentioned previously. To repeat, then, if you choose income-stock investing remember that earnings and prospects are more dynamic

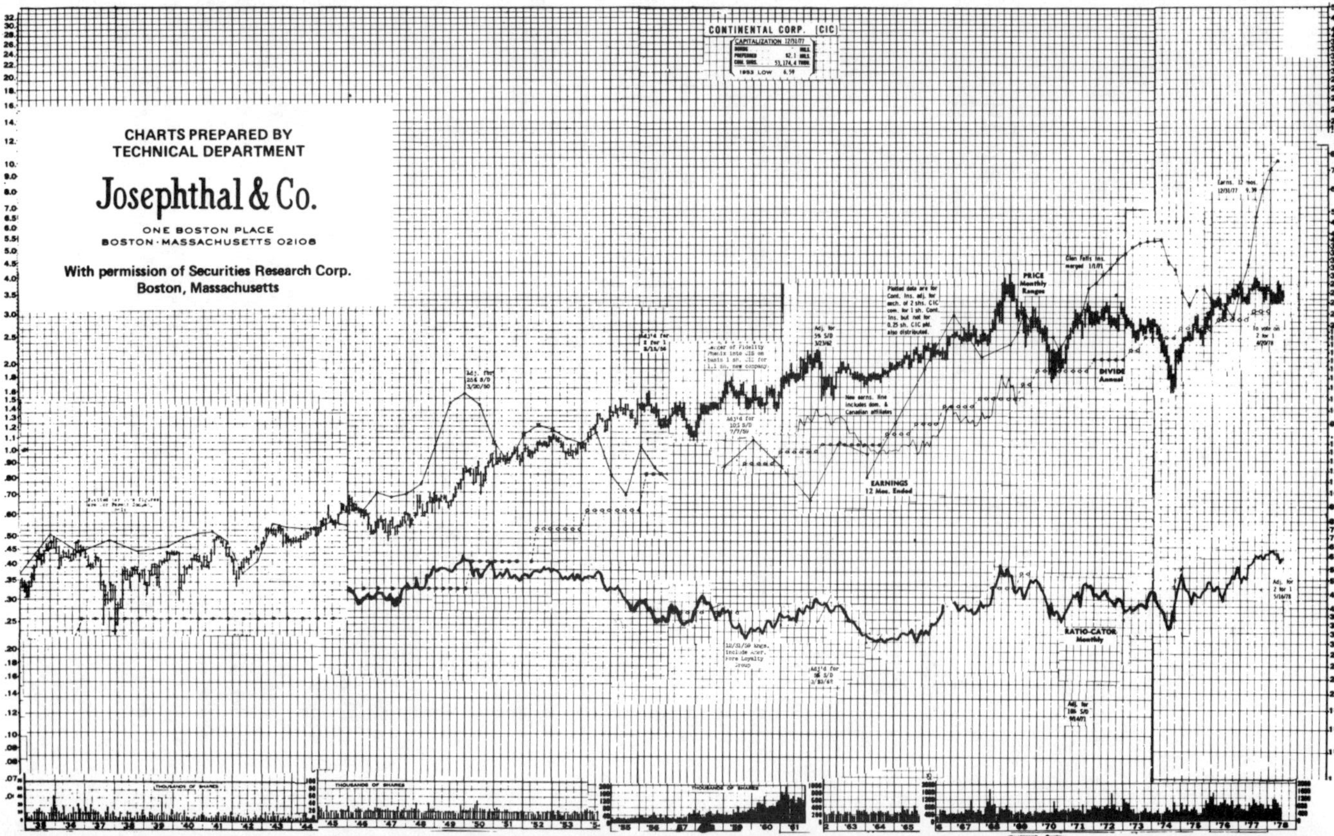

CHARTS PREPARED BY
TECHNICAL DEPARTMENT
Josephthal & Co.
ONE BOSTON PLACE
BOSTON · MASSACHUSETTS 02108
With permission of Securities Research Corp.
Boston, Massachusetts
CONTINENTAL CORP. (CIC)
CAPITALIZATION 12/31/77
1953 LOW 6.59
PRICE
Monthly
Ranges
EARNINGS
12 Mos. Ended
DIVIDE
Annual
RATIO-CATOR
Monthly
Glen Falls Ins. merged 1/1/71
THOUSANDS OF SHARES

and powerful influences on stock behavior than the dividends paid.

There is nothing more satisfying than investing in a low price/earnings stock and watching it advance sharply in price. There is also the prospect that along the way, there will be an upward re-evaluation of the P/E multiple leading to a further spectacular rise. This is the dream and hope of most low P/E buyers. They spend considerable time searching out companies that possess the characteristics for reappraisal. However, just as with turn-around companies, the success ratio is low. It takes a keen sense of industry competitive forces, company fundamentals, and patience to master the form of low P/E investing.

Instead, most people seek out low P/E on the belief that they are "safer" or "cheaper" than high P/E stocks. Being cheaper, performance over time is thought to stand a better chance of showing above-average results. Popularity of this investment philosophy was at its highest in the 1960-1965 period with the publication of studies done by S. Francis Nicholson in 1960, Paul Miller of the then Drexel and Co. in 1963, and the Continental Illinois Bank in 1965. All of these studies indicated that the lowest price/earnings ratio stocks dramatically out-performed the higher price/earnings ratio stocks. There still are many strong supporters today.

While the results of all of these studies were impressive, it must be pointed out that the period observed, the early to mid-1930s to the early 1960s, was one of generally rising price/earnings ratios. This was especially the case in the 1950-1962 period. More recent studies on the "efficient market" would tend to indicate that most stocks are "priced right" on any given day and, therefore, the odds of upward P/E reevaluations are very long indeed. Put a different way, stocks do not as a rule sell very far out of line with popular appraisal of their values. Before a buyer concludes that a stock is cheap, he should find out the reason, if any, why others have not also found it cheap and bid it up. There may be no true reason, except that the individual has been more observant than the public. Unfortunately, however, in most cases it will be found that there are definite reasons for low price/earnings ratios. In other words, you usually get what you pay for.

Worse yet, low P/E stocks do not necessarily protect you in falling markets. For example, in the 1974 market break, CIT Financial, despite modestly rising earnings *and* dividends and sporting a P/E of only ten times at the high, declined 55% as shown on the chart on page 43. The DJIA over the same period dropped 35%.

True, there were special factors weighing on CIT, such as a money panic, but scores of other low P/E stocks also showed substantial declines. The point here is that other factors, namely, earnings and prospects (just as with income stocks), are more powerful and important than simply a low P/E ratio. However, if your personality traits and experience (remember chapters I and II) indicate

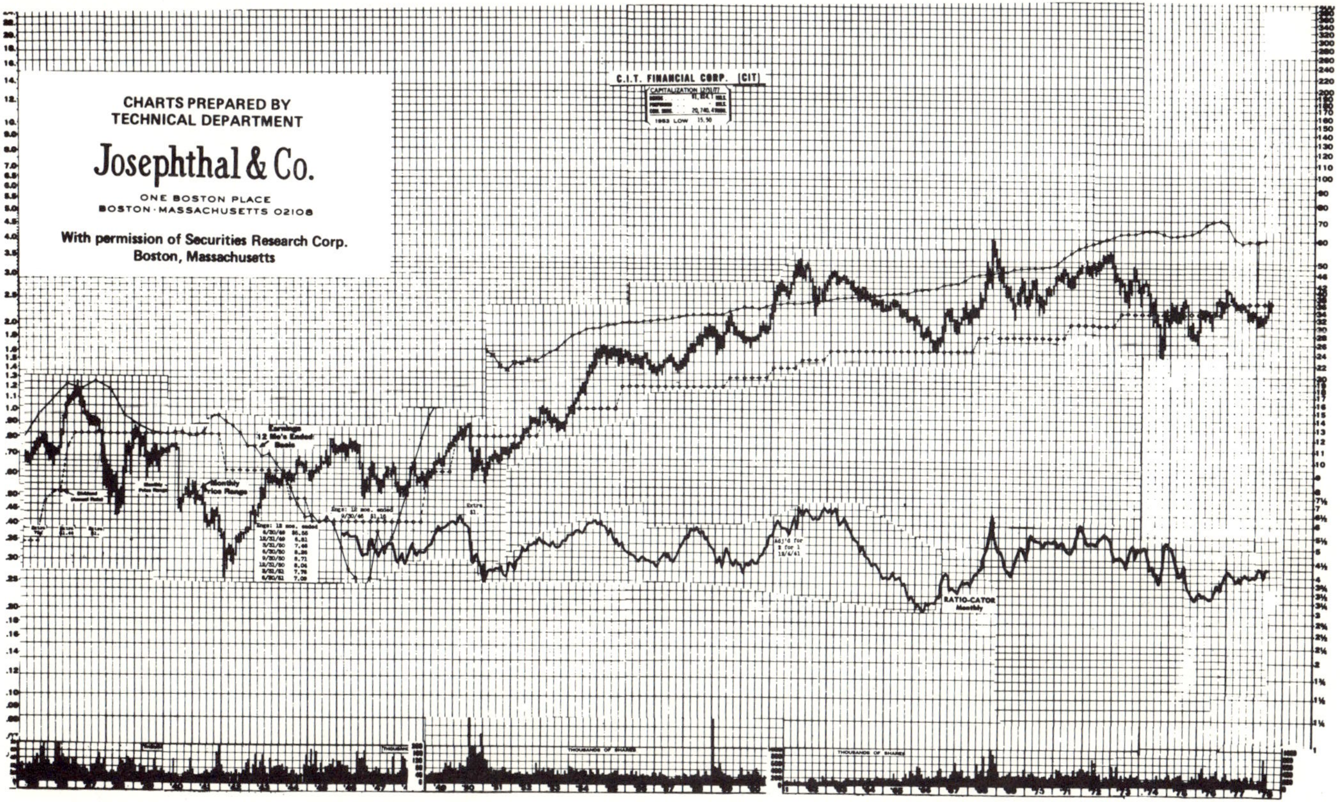
CHARTS PREPARED BY
TECHNICAL DEPARTMENT
Josephthal & Co.
ONE BOSTON PLACE
BOSTON · MASSACHUSETTS 02108
With permission of Securities Research Corp.
Boston, Massachusetts
C.I.T. FINANCIAL CORP. (CIT)
1963 LOW 15.50
Earnings
12 Mo's Ended
Basis
Monthly
Price Range
Extra
$1.
Adj'd for
2 for 1
12/4/41
RATIO-CATOR
Monthly
THOUSANDS OF SHARES
THOUSANDS OF SHARES

this is the best methodology for you, then by all means go ahead. Remember, though, it's earnings and prospects that count.

4. GROWTH-STOCK INVESTING

One of the most popular and widely followed investment philosophies is growth-stock investing. And no wonder! The mathematics are overwhelming and convincing. Here, investors are trying to isolate companies that show rapid earnings increases, operate in growth industries, and are generally immune to the business cycle. Furthermore, they are companies that have a protected or unique position because of patents, technology, superior marketing, industry position, or management expertise. This combination of characteristics, if it can produce a continuous stream of earnings, can do wondrous things to stock prices. The table below shows the effects of compounding, and explains Wall Street's enthusiasm for growth companies.

Company Growth Rate (Annual)	*Current Price per Share*	*Earnings per Share*	*Price/ Earnings Ratio*	*Years to Double Earnings*	*Theoretical Market Value at End of Period**	*Preser Value c Column at 10% Discou Rate*
Company A 5%	$10.00	$1.00	10-1	14.21	$20.00	$ 5.1
Company B 10%	$10.00	$1.00	10-1	7.27	$20.00	$10.0
Company C 15%	$10.00	$1.00	10-1	4.96	$20.00	$12.4

*Assuming no change in P/E ratios.

Develop an Investment Methodology

Financial literature is full of stories of how $10,000 invested in IBM in 1950 would be worth $553,500 at the end of 1975. Or $10,000 invested in American Home Products over the same period would be worth $389,204. They are great stories (particularly if you were a holder), but they're not meaningful to the average investor. He may feel it was just "luck" or the initial investment was far greater than he could afford. Well, the investment counseling firm of David L. Babson & Co., Inc., put together a study of growth versus income stocks twenty-one years ago to answer the question whether growth or income stocks produce the greater investment return over a period of years. Babson's staff put together two $10,000 portfolios each containing ten issues with a market value of $1,000 each. As shown in the table below, one list consisted entirely of "growth" stocks and the other solely of "income" stocks.

INCOME AND GROWTH PORTFOLIO
December 31, 1950

Income Stocks	*Growth Stocks*
American Telephone	Abbott Laboratories
American Brands	Celanese
Beneficial Corp.	Corning
Consolidated Edison	Dow
CPC International	Eastman Kodak
GATX	Exxon
General Foods	Gulf Oil
Interco	IBM
Warner-Lambert	Minnesota Mining
Woolworth	Union Carbide

On the next two pages are the updated results of the Babson portfolio to mid-1976. Both lists have produced excellent results. Nonetheless, there is a marked difference in the values. As most investors would assume, the growth portfolio has shown more capital appreciation. Against the original $10,000 commitment, its market value as of June 29, 1976, was $158,114. In contrast, the income list was worth $37,855. Just as striking is the difference in the present income-paying ability of the two portfolios. The ten growth stocks, which back in 1950 yielded less, now provide an annual return on cost of 42.1%, more than twice the 19.4 yield at cost of the income shares. Since 1950, the growth portfolio has provided a total investment return of $204,318 ($158,114 in capital appreciation and $46,204 in dividends).

Remember the little old lady or country club type from chapter I? Well, this is why they are rich—someone, somewhere, bought good growth stocks and they were never sold.

If it's that simple, why isn't everyone on Wall Street a millionaire? Just as with the other three investment approaches, growth-stock investing has its pitfalls. First, the identification of a "true" growth stock is not easy, except in hindsight. Then again, there are many issues masquerading as growth stocks which take in the unknowing investor. Managements know that consistent and rapidly expanding earnings bring high multiples. This makes stock options valuable, and acquisition policies viable, as well as other corporate objectives.

CURRENT MARKET VALUE

COMPARATIVE PERFORMANCE
GROWTH VS. INCOME PORTFOLIO
1950-1976

Growth Portfolio

Period	*Market Value*	*Annual Income*	*Yield at Market*	*Yield at Cost*
Average-1950	$ 10,000	$ 450	4.5%	4.5%
12/31/55	26,700	610	2.3	6.1
12/31/60	65,600	980	1.5	9.8
12/31/65	96,500	1,800	1.9	18.0
12/30/66	104,300	1,910	1.8	19.1
12/29/67	139,436	1,988	1.4	19.9
12/31/68	140,444	2,196	1.6	22.0
12/31/69	146,301	2,425	1.7	24.3
12/31/70	129,817	2,681	2.1	26.8
12/31/71	147,488	2,809	1.9	28.1
12/29/72	186,664	2,858	1.5	28.6
12/31/73	152,432	3,046	2.0	30.5
12/31/74	98,169	3,556	3.6	35.6
12/31/75	138,599	4,084	2.9	40.8
6/30/76	158,114	4,212*	2.7	42.1

Cumulative Income 1950-1976 = $46,204
*Indicated Annual Rate

Growth vs. Income Portfolio (continued)

Income Portfolio

Period	*Market Value*	*Annual Income*	*Yield at Market*	*Yield at Cost*
Average-1950	$10,000	$ 581	5.8%	5.8%
12/31/55	15,900	730	4.6	7.3
12/30/60	29,600	970	3.3	9.7
12/31/65	43,700	1,330	3.0	13.3
12/30/66	35,400	1,380	3.9	13.8
12/29/67	35,934	1,398	3.9	14.0
12/31/68	45,200	1,449	3.2	14.5
12/31/69	42,484	1,481	3.5	14.8
12/31/70	45,610	1,514	3.3	15.1
12/31/71	50,180	1,569	3.1	15.7
12/29/72	51,103	1,587	3.1	15.9
12/31/73	40,309	1,667	4.1	16.7
12/31/74	26,753	1,686	6.3	16.9
12/31/75	36,162	1,785	4.9	17.8
6/30/76	37,855	1,940*	5.1	19.4

Cumulative Income 1950-1976 = $31,498
*Indicated Annual Rate

For example, in the mid-1960s, Litton Industries was considered a glamorous growth situation and investors bid the shares up in price. Management used the stock's high price/earnings ratio to acquire a number of companies in the food, machinery, shipbuilding, and electronics industries. But was Litton really a growth company, or was management riding the crest of favorable circumstances until the bubble burst? Note on the chart Litton's earnings and price performance. Earnings went steadily up until 1967 when a number of ill-conceived acquisitions in low growth and cyclical industries began to cause the company some problems. Earnings plummeted and the stock went into a steady decline.

Second, even if you have identified a bona fide growth company like Johnson and Johnson, the market can overexploit a good thing. The investor who paid fifty times earnings for JNJ in 1974 received the equivalent of 2% (excluding dividends) on his money—not a good return in anyone's book. In other words, the purchase price of a growth stock is just as important as the earnings record of the company.

Third, how do you know when your growth favorite has stopped growing and has changed characteristics? General Foods was considered a blue-chip growth stock in the decade of the 1950s as per capita consumption of coffee expanded. The stock performed like a superstar. Like JNJ, enthusiasm got carried away in 1961 and despite moderate earnings progress, share prices went no-

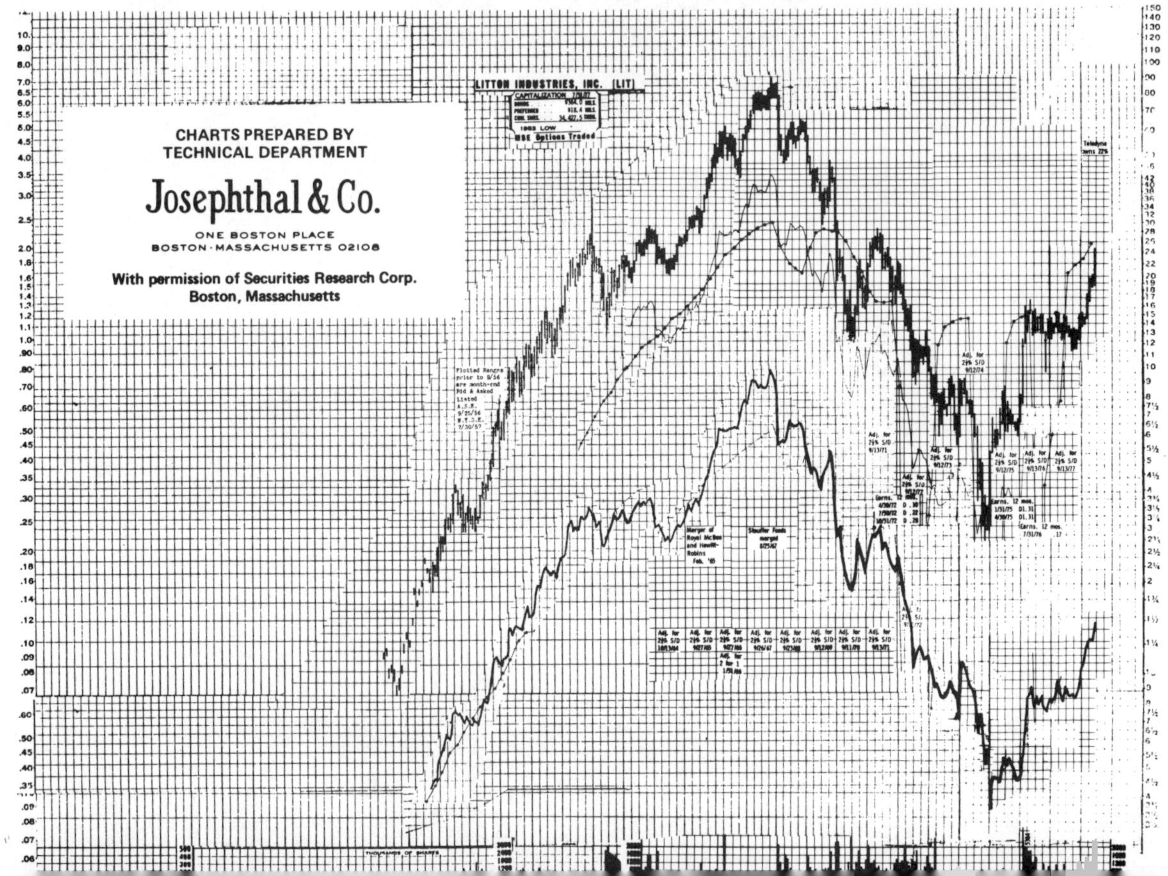

CHARTS PREPARED BY
TECHNICAL DEPARTMENT
Josephthal & Co.
ONE BOSTON PLACE
BOSTON · MASSACHUSETTS 02108
With permission of Securities Research Corp.
Boston, Massachusetts
LITTON INDUSTRIES, INC. (LIT)
NSE Options Traded
Teledyne owns 22%
Plotted Ranges prior to 9/56 are month-end Bid & Asked
Merger of Royal McBee and Hewitt-Robins Feb. '65
Stouffer Foods merged
THOUSANDS OF SHARES

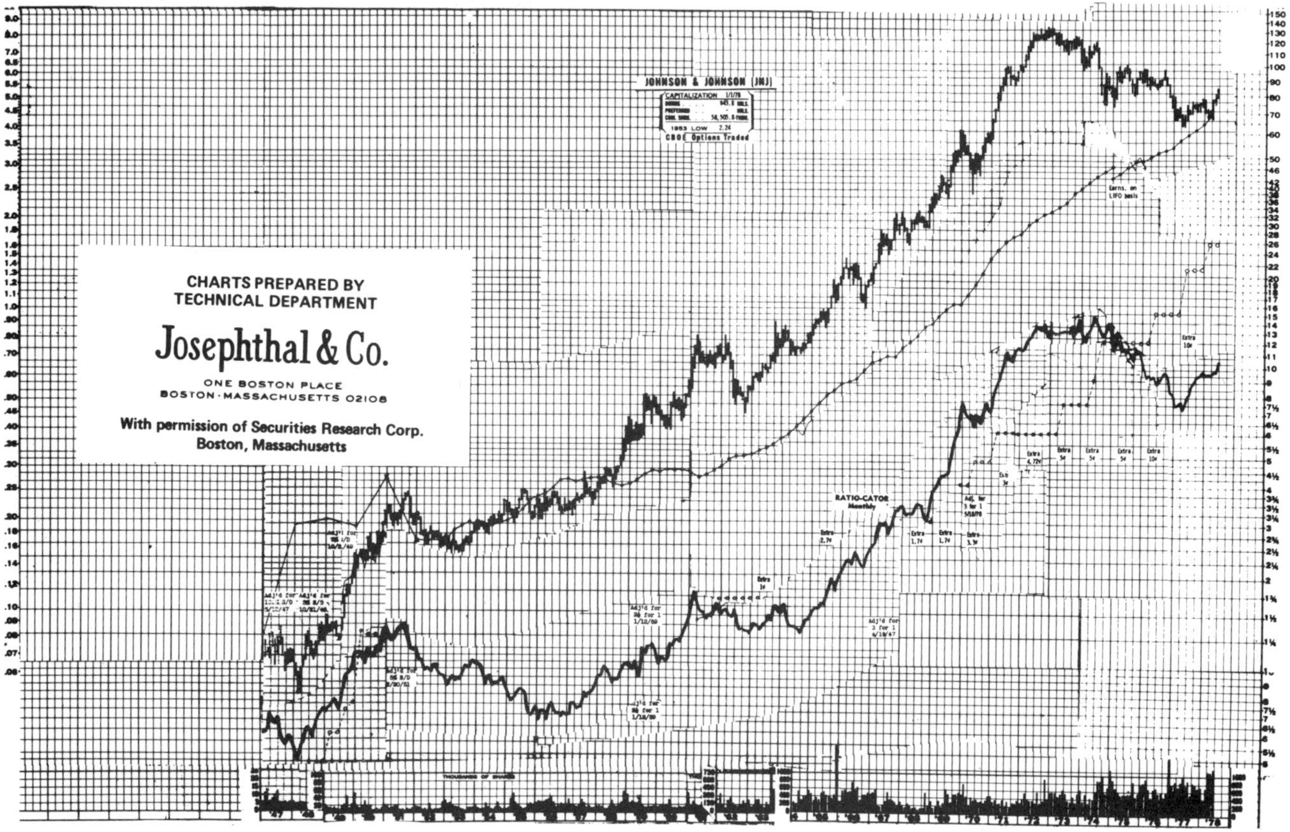
JOHNSON & JOHNSON (JNJ)
CAPITALIZATION 1/1/78
1953 LOW 2.24
CBOE Options Traded
Earns. on LIFO basis
RATIO-CATOR Monthly
CHARTS PREPARED BY TECHNICAL DEPARTMENT
Josephthal & Co.
ONE BOSTON PLACE
BOSTON · MASSACHUSETTS 02108
With permission of Securities Research Corp.
Boston, Massachusetts
THOUSANDS OF SHARES

where. But by 1968, it became apparent that General Foods growth had slowed to a crawl and its stock price finally tumbled in 1971.

Fourth, it is more difficult to know when a slowdown in the growth rate is temporary, and when a return to "trend line" growth will take place. Like General Foods, Procter & Gamble was a growth favorite in the 1950s, became overexploited in 1962, saw its growth rate slow down in 1964 and 1965. However, growth resumed in 1966.

Just as in other fields, knowledge, experience, consistency, and *patience* are needed for success. Psychological problems also exist with growth-stock investing. Wide price swings can cause anxiety at the wrong time. Stocks tend to get overpriced quickly and the temptation to sell is great. People who do sell often think they are smarter than the market and can employ other strategies such as "buy low"—"sell high" to the growth-stock approach. If you can master the discipline of the growth-stock approach and have a good sense of value combined with strong nerves at times, then the power of compounding can work for you.

Now that I have described four investment approaches you can combine your experience from your experimental fund together with your personality traits to form your own personal investment methodology. As I mentioned earlier, there is no one way to make money. There are literally dozens of approaches, as well as variations, permutations, or combinations of the four already described. Some people prefer to concentrate their

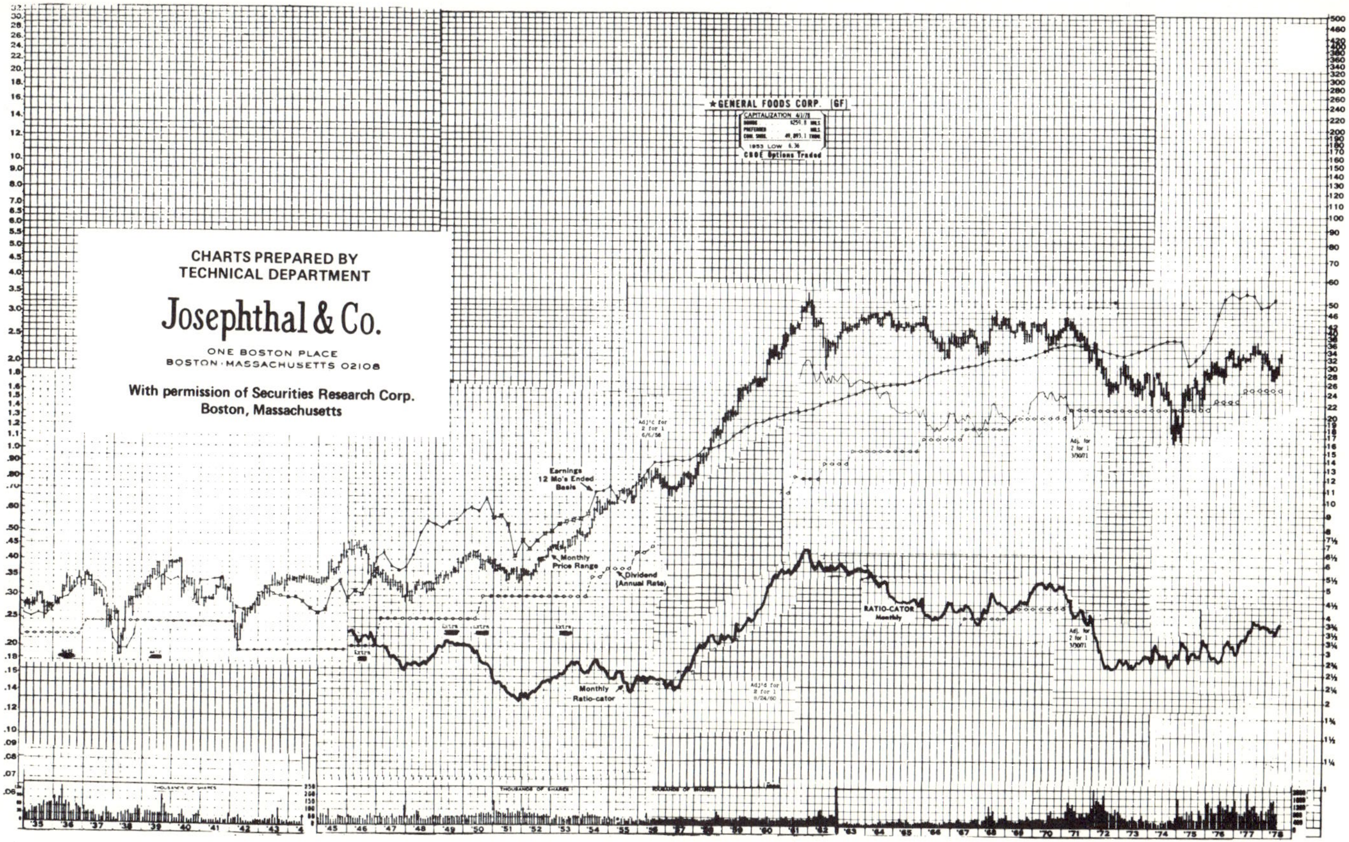
★GENERAL FOODS CORP. (GF)
CAPITALIZATION 4/1/78
1953 LOW 6.36
CBOE Options Traded
CHARTS PREPARED BY
TECHNICAL DEPARTMENT
Josephthal & Co.
ONE BOSTON PLACE
BOSTON · MASSACHUSETTS 02108
With permission of Securities Research Corp.
Boston, Massachusetts
Earnings
12 Mo's Ended
Basis
Monthly
Price Range
Dividend
(Annual Rate)
Monthly
Ratio-cator
RATIO-CATOR
Monthly
Adj. for
2 for 1
3/30/71
Extra
THOUSANDS OF SHARES
'35
'36
'37
'38
'39
'40
'41
'42
'43
'45
'46
'47
'48
'49
'50
'51
'52
'53
'54
'55
'56
'57
'58
'59
'60
'61
'62
'63
'64
'65
'66
'67
'68
'69
'70
'71
'72
'73
'74
'75
'76
'77
'78

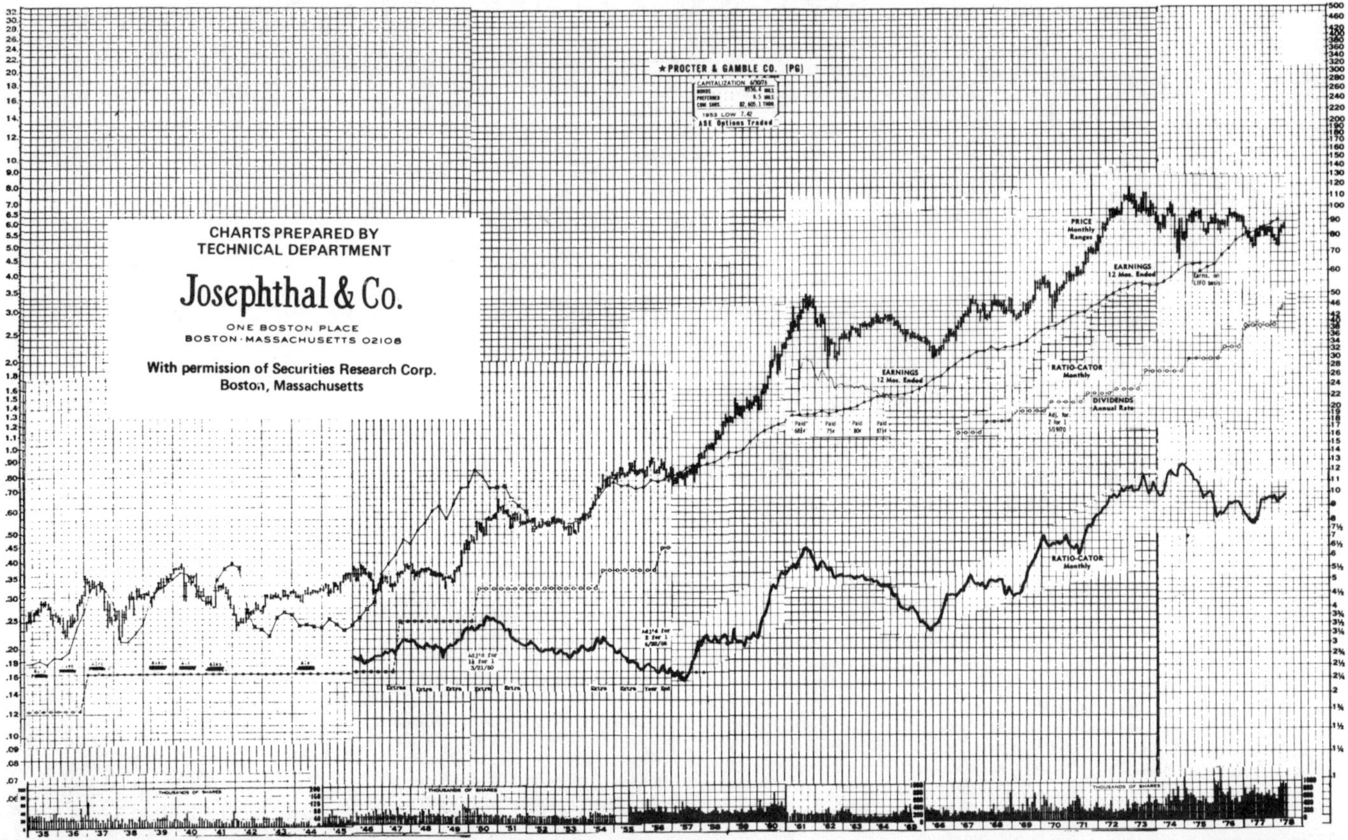
★PROCTER & GAMBLE CO. (PG)
CAPITALIZATION 6/30/76
1953 LOW 7.42
ASE Options Traded
CHARTS PREPARED BY
TECHNICAL DEPARTMENT
Josephthal & Co.
ONE BOSTON PLACE
BOSTON · MASSACHUSETTS 02108
With permission of Securities Research Corp.
Boston, Massachusetts
PRICE
Monthly
Ranges
EARNINGS
12 Mos. Ended
RATIO-CATOR
Monthly
DIVIDENDS
Annual Rate
THOUSANDS OF SHARES

energies on emerging companies, hoping to hit another Xerox or Polaroid. Others emphasize only technology companies. Whatever method you choose, make sure it suits you and you stay "true" to your philosophy, but be systematic, consistent, and disciplined.

IV

TYING IT ALL TOGETHER

An anonymous prophet of the market once said, "A good speculation is always a good investment. A poor investment is never a good speculation." The dividing line between investment and speculation is very thin, since both must be grounded in sound principles. The truth is there is no investment which doesn't involve some risk and is not something of a gamble. The difference is essentially the amount of risk assumed. What we can try to do perhaps is to come to a better understanding of how to reduce the element of risk in your undertaking.

The first three chapters have attempted to provide the proper basis for a successful investment program through realistic goal-setting (motivation), knowing yourself (psychological and emotional factors), and the development of a methodology or philosophy (achieving goals) to provide the framework for the consistent, systematic, and disciplined application of investment principles. Your eventual success will be governed by your abilities, the stakes you possess, the time you devote, the risks you assume, and the market climate in which you operate. I have encouraged the use of a small amount of money for experimentation before embarking upon a full-scale investment program. While reading and studying help, I firmly believe knowledge from actual experience is the answer to why one profits, while lack of it is the reason why one loses. I have often noticed that we rarely benefit from other people's mistakes. It seems it makes us more eager to try to do the same thing. Maybe this is because all of us want to "beat the game" and show ourselves to be smarter than the other fellow. In any case, it is only after we have repeated the errors of others that their instructive lessons sink home. In addition, making money in the market demands a certain amount of flair. No amount of study or practice can make you successful in the handling of capital if you're really not cut out for it.

Mastery of the three stepping-stones to success requires time and devotion. In fact, I call goal-setting, knowing yourself, and methodology the Holy Trinity of investments. Inside the triangle is knowledge and experience. Without proper goals, you cannot be properly motivated, you cannot assess the proper amount of risk to assume. You lack direction and point of reference or measure-

ment. Remember, I said investing is a serious business. Treat it as such. You have to really want to make money. If you are like the characters in chapter I, you're just kidding yourself. Investing is work! You should plan to spend at least an hour or two every night reading, researching, and reflecting.

The second leg—know yourself—conditions you to be as objective as possible. You have to know your limitations, and strengthen your strong traits. This is extremely important. Since most people do not have the time or aptitude to spend on the stock market, the task of determining what is going on in the market and economy at any particular time is reserved for government officials, magazine editors, newspaper reporters, financial writers, and brokers. Their pronouncements on the state of the economy or the condition of the stock market are generally believed and acted upon by the majority of the investing public. Yet, these very same pronouncements are probably already reflected in current prices. Instead, a good investor must predict the future and act before it occurs. He must search through a mass of information for the significant facts. He must then act dispassionately and skillfully on the basis of the facts before him.

What makes the task of fact-finding so difficult is that in the stock market the facts of any given situation come to us through a curtain of human emotions. The often violent swings of stock prices are not caused by impersonal economic forces or changing events, but by the human reactions to these happenings. The constant problem of the investor is how to separate the cold, hard economic facts from the warm feeling of the people dealing with these facts. Few tasks are more difficult. The main obstacle rests in disentangling ourselves from our own emotions. I can recall an experience of my own that highlights this problem. As a young analyst, I had recommended Corn Products (now CPC International) on the basis of a resumption in the company's growth trend. A considerable amount of stock was purchased on the basis of my recommendation. In my preparation for a management interview with the Corporate Vice President of Finance, I noticed the company was embarking upon a large capital expenditure program to increase wet corn milling capacity. The problem was that companies such as Standard Brands, A. E. Staly, and National Starch were doing the same. When I questioned this vice president, he assured me that there was nothing to worry about. While I still had an uneasy feeling after the interview, I did nothing because I wanted to believe him. Within three months, prices broke; I never forgot the lessons of that episode.

A sound methodology is the bedrock of the successful investor. It ties everything together. It forms the model of how or by what means you are going to achieve your goals. Again, there is no right or wrong investment philosophy—just many ways to make money. An investment methodology is the only way I know to force you to consistently apply investment techniques. You can adopt one of the four investment methodologies described earlier, or you can adopt a combination. The point is, it should suit your style—your way of doing things.

In the center of this triangle is knowledge and experience. Both are essential ingredients to success. Both build confidence, the all-important trait that will give you the courage to act on your own convictions and stand apart from the crowd. Knowledge will expand your mind, keep you fresh, flexible, and open to new thoughts. Chapter VIII contains a beginning reading list. I suggest that you add additional titles and create your own library. Experience is the best teacher if the lessons are clearly learned. Unfortunately, most people continually make the same mistakes. By consciously trying to embody the characteristics essential for a successful investor, while maintaining a well-thought-out investment philosophy geared to your personality, you will reduce your errors and be on the road to profitable investing. Remember, there are no easy answers, no formulas, no black boxes which lead to riches in the market. The market is a game of probabilities and it is my belief the thoughts expressed in the first three chapters will increase your chances for success.

V

SERVICES, CHARTS, AND ALL THAT JAZZ

There is probably no other subject about which more has been written with so little meaning as the stock market. Anyone who buys or sells a stock, anyone who owns a stock, is ready to bury you in a mass of meaningless market observations. The newspapers will give five reasons why the market went up or down on a particular day. Free advice abounds everywhere. Even worse, the market has many prophets who sell their dubious advice. That these messiahs survive and multiply is testimony to the great gullibility of the public. As soon as a professional prophet rents advertising space in a leading financial publication to tell all how he "called the turn," the dollars flow to Mecca. By the time the next "turn" is past, a new evangelist is in the headlines to tell how he did what nobody else could do. This vicious cycle will endure so long as the market is based upon the mass decisions of a largely uninformed public. Lately, the market prophet has gained a new degree of sophistication—he is intoxicated with the theory of contrary opinion. Anything on which anybody agrees can't be true.

When it comes to the stock market, truth is often so elusive and distorted that it may as well not exist—that is, except for those who can coldly and logically distinguish the emotional from the factual, the real from the unreal. My point is that this is no easy task. It takes much hard work and study, much knowledge of the market psychology, knowledge that surefire systems just don't work.

In my years of experience, I've seen advisors come and go. What they print and have to say rarely is worth the time of reading. They usually play up on your sense of fear or greed for their appeal. Many are always bearish or always bullish, even when the trend is clearly against them. Just pick up the paper. "Sixty Current Buy-Recommendations," "Is the Gold Panic Over?" "Low-Priced Action Leaders," "Uraniums, to Double," "Bullish or Bearish?" "Silver: Boom or Bust?" "How the Young Millionaires Trade Commodities."

I'm most skeptical of the investment services which tell people "what stocks to buy and sell and when." These buy-this-today-and-sell-that-tomorrow services usually don't stay in business for long simply because their record over the years is never really any good. I have many friends who have consistently made money in the market over the years by buying values at roughly the right time and selling at roughly the right time. But services that tell you to buy IBM at 200 and sell it next year at 300 just don't last. That's because they're offering people a simple recipe, a cookbook formula —a pipe dream. The real message repeated many times before in this book is that each man has to learn and develop his own way of operating in the stock market. What works for you will not work for your neighbor, because your neighbor doesn't think or act the way you do.

This doesn't mean that all services are bad. A few have withstood the test of time. Typically, services can be divided into two categories—those providing opinion and those providing facts (they may give their interpretations along with the facts). I have always preferred services which provide the facts, and I supply my own interpretations. You may have a different style and prefer the opinion services as a foil to your own independent thought process. That judgment must be yours, as must be the selection of what you consider a "good" service. I would suggest experimentation. Don't be afraid to take up the "get acquainted" offers. Spend a few dollars and take some trial subscriptions. You will find the experience worthwhile. You may find just the service for you or you may end up sharing my cynicism.

Others have come to depend upon charts and

technicians. Technical analysis has been called everything from the chart players art to the Braille system of forecasting. However, for those who devote all their time to the subject, it is an exceedingly complex study of the combination of forces that shape trends in security prices. In a sense, it is an environmental approach to the market. To the technician, stock price movements are determined by intrinsic worth (fundamental value) and what the investment community thinks they are worth. This latter factor is the psychological element in stock prices that accounts for many of the wide swings. This particular area is one of the major subjects of study by the technical analyst. In other words, in addition to asking why and how much, the technical analyst wants to know who. Is the demand (buying) or supply (selling) public or professional, scattered or concentrated? How responsive is price to demand? One of the technician's basic tenets is that at bottoms, stocks are bought by the few (informed) and sold by the many (uninformed), and at tops, they are sold by the few and bought by the many.

Technical analysis is historical and evolutionary. It is historical in that it studies past market behavior (price and volume) to determine trend patterns in such parameters as price, volume, relative strength, momentum, and volatility. It is evolutionary to the extent it attempts to relate all the factors that determine these trend patterns in order to arrive at a judgment of future performance. These factors are as fundamental to the technician as earnings and dividends are to the security analyst.

Charts have an important place in the technician's bag of tricks. To the uninformed they look like the easy way to success in the market. Remember there are no easy ways! To the technician, charts are really a beginning or confirming tool rather than a sole means to an end.

Do they work? Certainly not the way most books on charting would lead you to believe. Whether the whole field of technical analysis is hocus-pocus is a real question. I'm impressed by the "random-walkers" whose research indicates that prices have no memory, and yesterday has nothing to do with tomorrow. In other words, on any given day, the chance of a stock moving up, or the stock moving down is fifty-fifty. This means that a past history of stock prices cannot be used to predict the future in any meaningful way. This goes against the heart of technical analysis.

Why then do some people persist in using charts or technical tools? I guess because deep down people really don't believe that the market is efficient at least in the short run. Maybe it has to do with the gambling instinct in all of us. Or worse yet, our egos tell us we can beat the market. I confess that I find charts and certain technical indicators useful. I have my reservations about their predictive powers, but they provide me with an important "crutch."

I can get a "feel" for mass opinion by scanning a book of charts. Better yet, it gives me a snapshot of the market at a given time. I can get an idea of its structure, relationships, and valuations—like a road map. I can then correlate this information with my own opinions and research. It is simply another tool used in my research process. In the final analysis, it's real events that count, not the lines and x's. It's knowledge and understanding of the discounting process. If charts and technical analysis help you in this process, it doesn't matter what the "random-walkers" say, it's what people believe and act upon that counts, at least in the short run. But remember the limitations. If charting really worked, everyone would be doing it. It's best to familiarize yourself with the jargon and read some books on the subject. Talk to some technicians to get an understanding of their mixture of truth and alchemy and then make up your own mind.

As I have so often said, there is no universal formula for making or investing money in the market. Traditional investment philosophy implies that values are constant and absolute—something from which one may stray, but to which he must inevitably return. But investment values are always changing and relative. It is necessary to avoid forming any patterns or preconceptions in investment thinking. The only "constant" in investing is the certainty of change. You need to evaluate change on its own terms and in its own time, rather than on terms belonging to some other time.

In the process, remember what Tallyrand once said, "There is somebody who knows more than anybody and that is everybody." So it is with the market. The movement of stock prices reflects all known facts—past, present, and future. These movements are not based on factual knowledge alone, but include emotional factors. The enthusiasm of investors will wax and wane around some theoretical norm, creating artificial values which operate only as long as the madness of the crowd remains blissfully unabated.

VI

DEVELOP YOUR OWN INDICATORS

If you're going to be independent and stand apart from the crowd, you will need help in reaching important decisions. Some people like to use valuation models. Others depend upon technical analysis, while still others rely on economic forecasting or the use of indicators.

I have eschewed the use of elaborate or complicated systems for valuations, and I have not relied solely upon economic forecasting or technical analysis. I place little weight on the fundamental business indicators. This may surprise you but the abysmal record of the leading economic forecasters speaks for itself. If they can't do better with their superior knowledge, equations, and computers and access to information, why should I pretend I can call the turn with any more clairvoyance? The use of elaborate systems for valuation models leaves me cold. They depend upon your ability to predict key variables which are interdependent and dynamic. As the chart opposite indicates, the extreme fluctuations in price/earnings multiples make this task difficult. The fundamental business indicators, such as retail sales, personal income, new orders, reflect the current state of business, while the stock market generally discounts a change in the trend of general business before it actually shows up in the indices of business. I would rather let my set of indicators and the market tell their own stories.

I prefer the use of some simple indicators which give me a feel for the state of the economy and market sentiment, as well as some idea of valuation or market level. I would suggest you find out what works best for you. As a starter, I would recommend an excellent publication called *Business Conditions Digest*, published by the Department of Commerce. Additionally, some of the books listed in chapter VIII provide excellent reference material.

My indicator approach allows me to achieve my main objective, which is the determination of the investment climate. You can't expect to swim upstream in a bear market or, conversely, it's costly to be bearish in a bull market. Since I believe the stock market is a financial phenomenon, and therefore a residual of the supply and demand for credit, I place considerable emphasis on monetary indi-

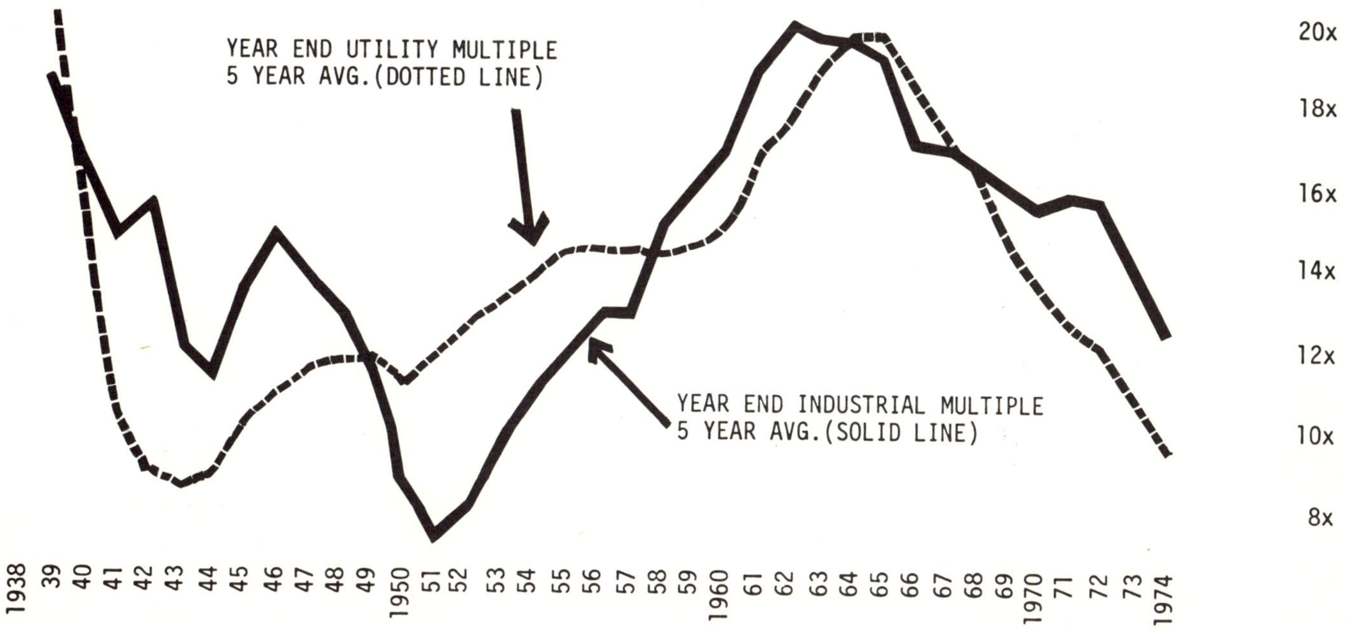
YEAR END UTILITY MULTIPLE
5 YEAR AVG. (DOTTED LINE)
YEAR END INDUSTRIAL MULTIPLE
5 YEAR AVG. (SOLID LINE)
20x
18x
16x
14x
12x
10x
8x
1938
39
40
41
42
43
44
45
46
47
48
49
1950
51
52
53
54
55
56
57
58
59
1960
61
62
63
64
65
66
67
68
69
1970
71
72
73
1974

cators. The reason for this lies in the interrelationship between the supply and demand for credit and the physical output of goods and services. All other things being equal, the supply and demand for credit will be just enough to finance the current production of goods and services. However, when the actual output of goods and services is low relative to the supply and demand for credit, recipients of money payments tend to invest in financial assets with their excess cash balances. As the production of goods and services increases relative to the supply and demand for credit, the amount of excess liquidity for the purchase of financial assets tends to decrease (or as the excess liquidity is converted into the production of goods and services, the amount available for the purchase of financial assets decreases). The Federal Reserve Board controls the supply of credit, primarily through open market operations, by providing the banking system with reserves to meet the demand for credit. Accordingly, as the chart opposite shows, the level and rate of change of excess reserves in the banking system has proven to be a very reliable stock market indicator. This series is widely published and is available in the *Business Conditions Digest*.

While the level and trend of member bank free reserves are good quantitative measures of both Federal Reserve policy and liquidity of the banking system, the money supply is the driving force of the economy. The money supply has an important influence on credit availability and interest rates,

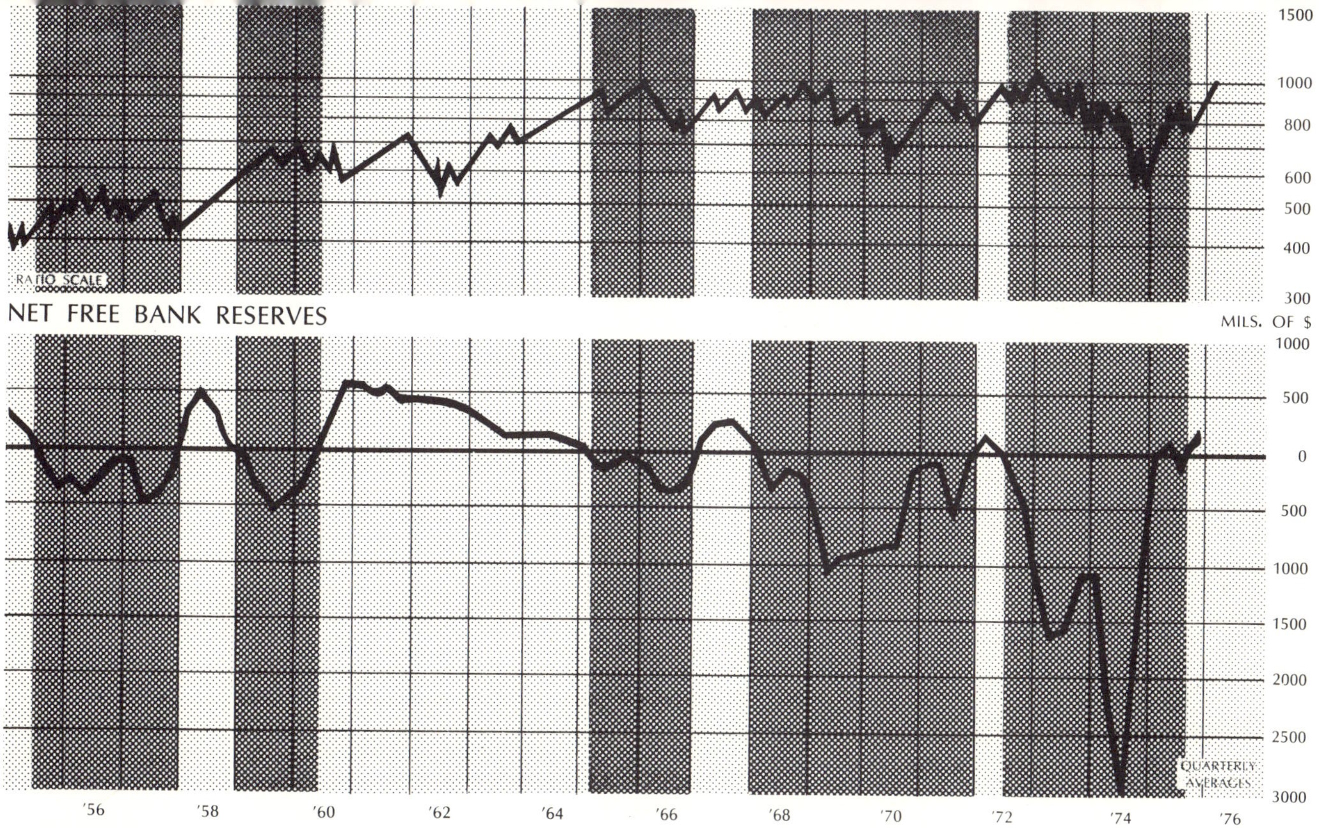

SHADED AREAS INDICATE PERIODS OF NET BORROWED RESERVES

SOURCES: DOW JONES COMPANY AND THE BOARD OF GOVERNORS OF THE FEDERAL RESERVE SYSTEM and therefore can either stimulate or restrict the economy and determine business prospects. The rate of change in money supply reflects the current momentum and future course of the overall economy, and these factors have historically been key ingredients for the trend and level of stock prices. Because of high inflation in recent years, I have used the money supply figures, adjusted for prices changes. The chart opposite is an illustration of how the rate of change in real money supply affected the trend of stock market prices.

For indicators of market psychology and sentiment, I like to use two technical tools—the monthly NYSE Short Interest Ratio and the Odd-Lot Short Interest Ratio. Both have good records of depicting periods of extreme pessimism and optimism, as illustrated in the accompanying charts.

The Short Interest Ratio is reported in *Barron's* (a weekly financial publication available at newsstands) and is the ratio of total NYSE Short Interest at the middle of a month divided by average daily trading volume for the corresponding period. A normal Short Interest Ratio is about 1.4 while a ratio above 1.8 is generally considered a sign of excessive pessimism. Conversely, a ratio of less than 1.0 is a warning of growing optimism and increasing risks.

The ratio of odd-lot short sales to odd-lot sales is shown on page 79. Many investors believe the odd-lot short seller is wrong most of the time; hence, the figures showing his activity are good indicators

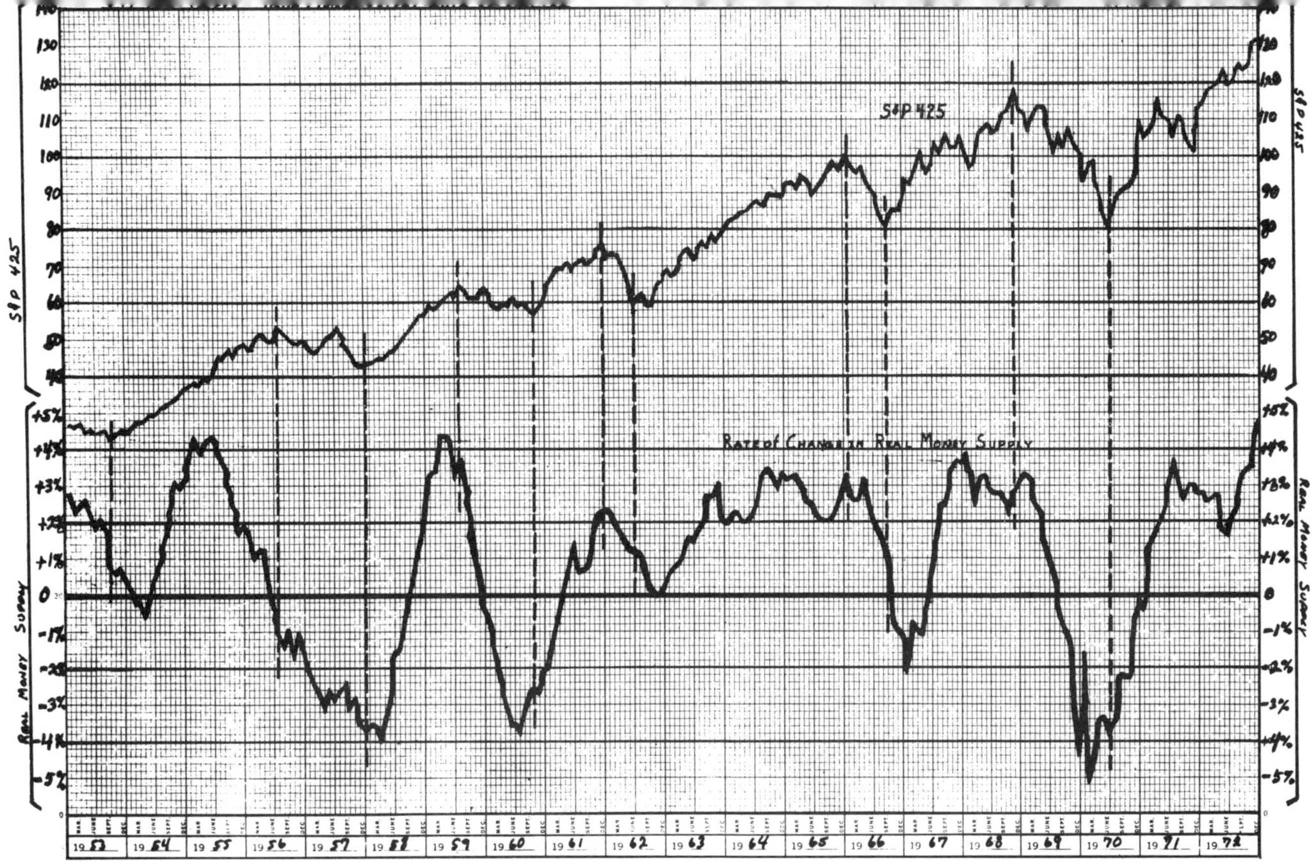
S&P 425
Real Money Supply
Rate of Change in Real Money Supply
140
130
120
110
100
90
80
70
60
50
40
+5%
+4%
+3%
+2%
+1%
0
-1%
-2%
-3%
-4%
-5%
1953
1954
1955
1956
1957
1958
1959
1960
1961
1962
1963
1964
1965
1966
1967
1968
1969
1970
1971
1972

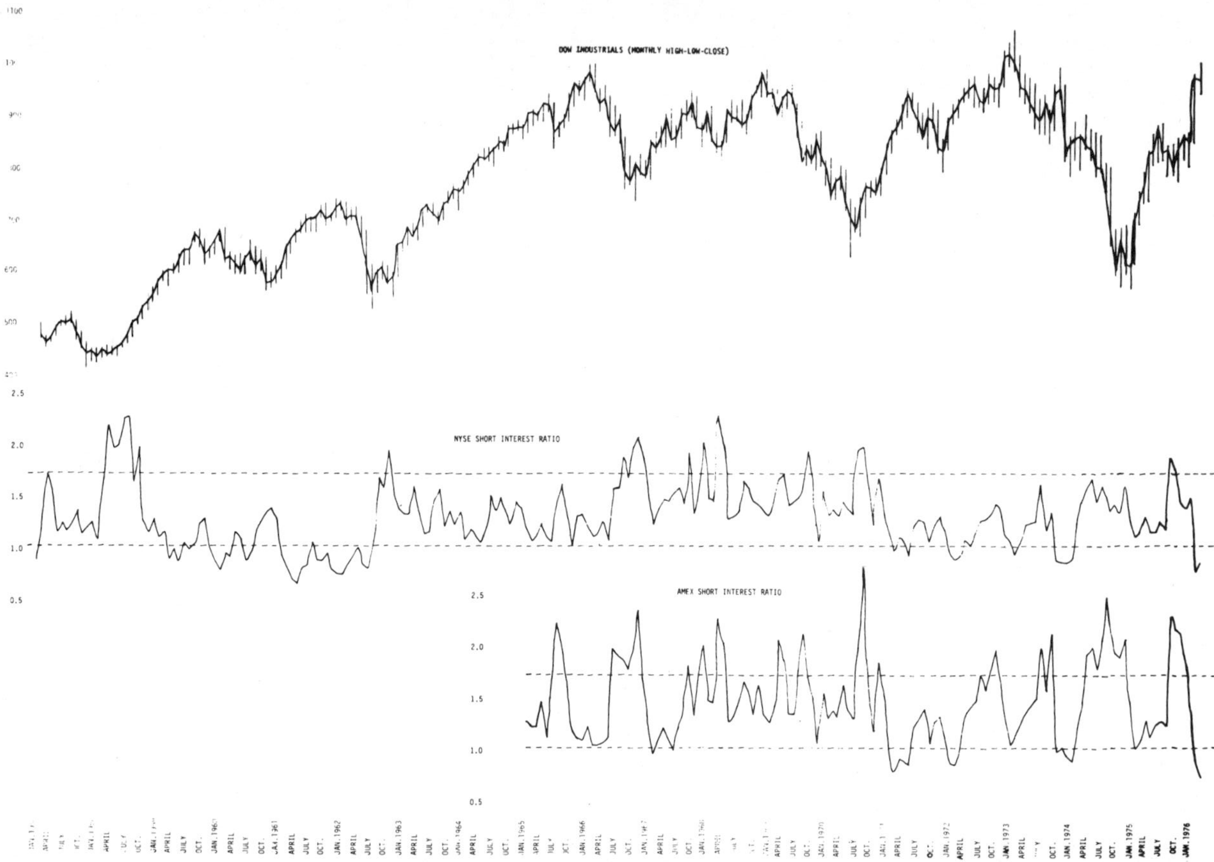

A comparison of the monthly short interest ratio for the NYSE and AMEX compared to the monthly

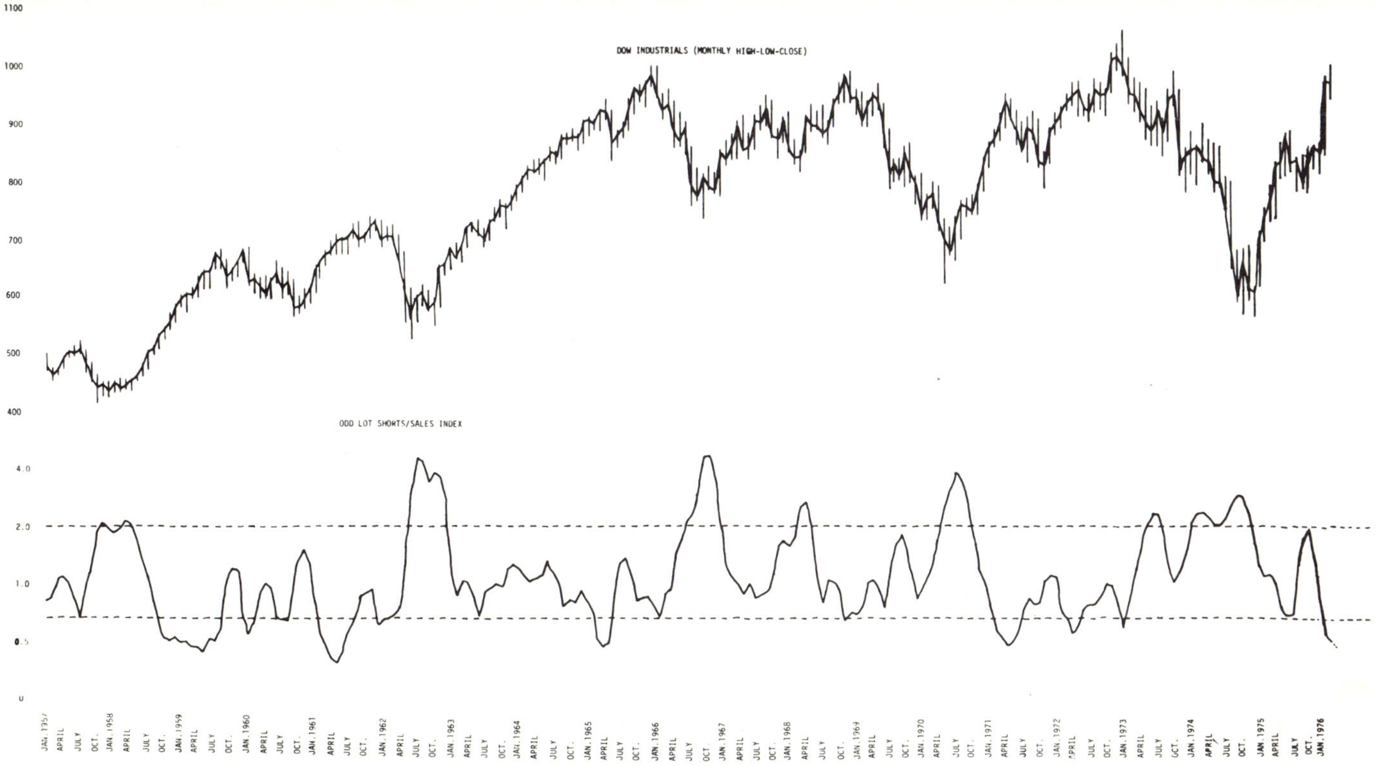

A comparison of a three-month average ratio of odd lot short sales to odd lot sales to the monthly Dow Jones Industrial Average shows excessive pessimism at a ratio of 2% or higher usually coinciding with market lows. Conversely, a sign of possible excessive optimism is found with a ratio below 0.7%.

of market sentiment. A reading of a ratio of 2 or higher is considered extremely bullish, as it indicates extreme pessimisim on the part of odd-lot short sellers. A ratio of .75 shows extreme optimism on the part of the odd-lot short seller and is cause for concern.

For indications of market and sentiment valuation, I use two very simple series: the yield on the DJIA and stock prices as a multiple of dividends. In chapter III, I point out that earnings, not dividend yield, are the key element in stock selection. However, in order to gain a broad perspective on the market as a whole, I use the dividend series.

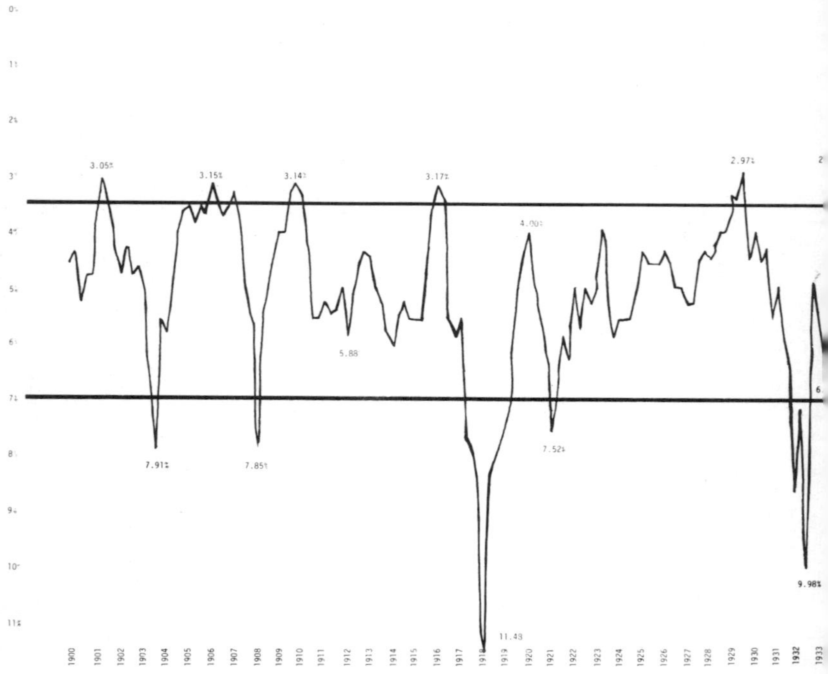

Dividends tend to be more stable than corporate profits and can be compared more easily with the bond market. These indicators have given very reliable signals without the investor's worrying about the trend of corporate profits or the appropriate price earnings ratio.

The chart below on the Dow Jones dividend yield shows that whenever stock yields get below 3.5%, market enthusiasm is likely to be high and there is reason for caution. Conversely, whenever yields approach 6% and pessimism is high, the market has probably "bottomed-out."

In addition to stock yields, stock prices as a

DOW JONES INDUSTRIAL AVERAGE DIVIDEND YIELD

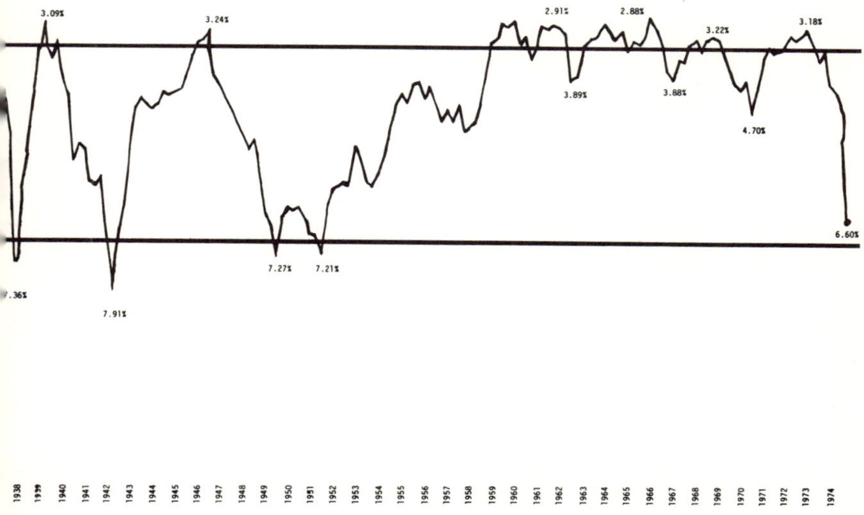

multiple of dividends have also shown a remarkable record of calling "turns" in the stock market.

You will see from the chart that extreme pessimism will occur when readings approach ten times. Readings of twenty-five times and higher have typically been associated with periods of optimism and excessive valuation. The fifty-year average of stock prices as a multiple of dividends has been about twenty-two times.

In order to place stock yields in proper perspective, the stock/bond ratio is useful. The stock/bond ratio is nothing more than the yield on equities divided by the yield on bonds. In other words, if stock and bond yields were the same, the stock/bond ratio would be 1/1. The diagram opposite shows the quarterly behavior of stock and bond yields and the ratio of yields in the equity market to those in the debt market for the last forty-eight years. Stock yields are calculated as the sum of dividends of all dividend-paying common stocks listed on the New York Stock Exchange divided by the sum of their prices and adjusted for the Standard and Poor's 500 Index on the day of calculation relative to its average for the month. The bond yield series is the Standard and Poor's corporate Aaa composite. By studying the trends in dividends, dividend payout ratios, equity prices, and interest rates, one can get a feel for the relative attractiveness of stocks versus bonds. This is particularly relevant in today's market as the bond market provides competition for the stock market.

STOCK PRICES AS MULTIPLES OF DIVIDENDS

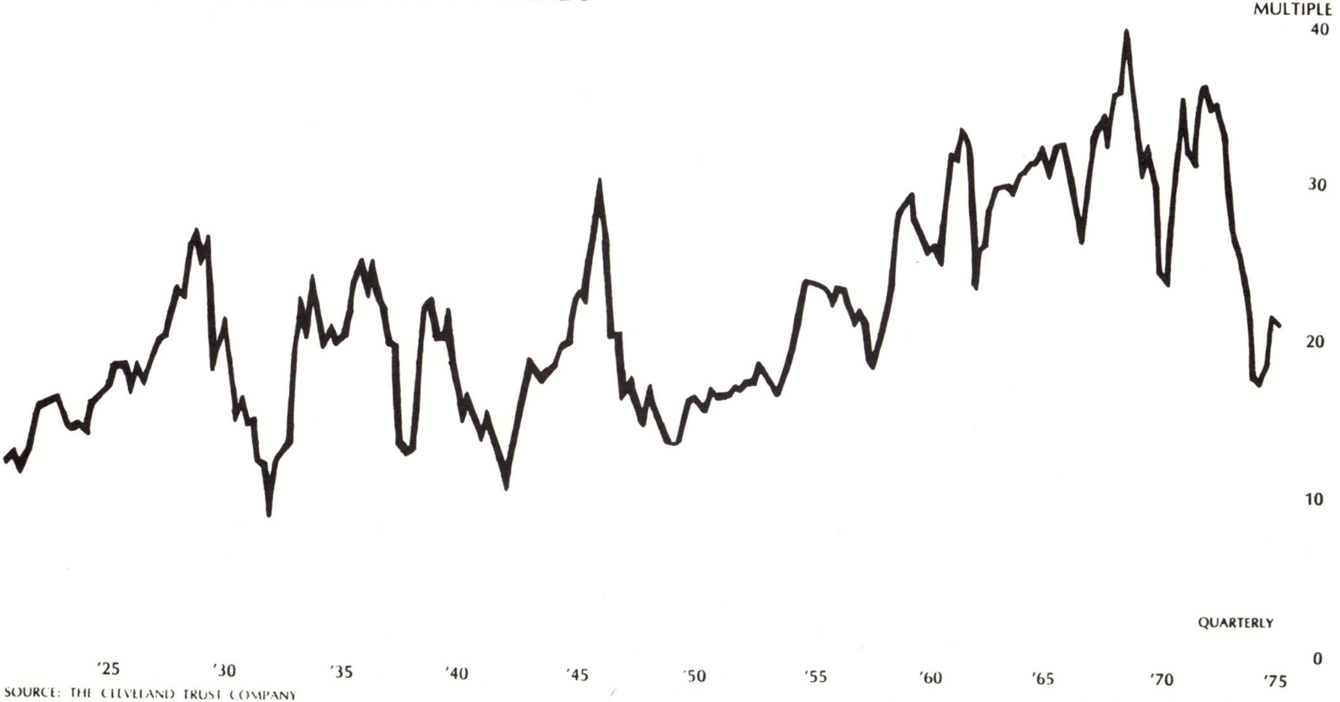

SOURCE: THE CLEVELAND TRUST COMPANY

	Common Stock Prices as Multiples of Dividends	*Common Stock Yields*
1925-34 Average	18.06	5.83
1935-44 Average	17.71	5.85
1945-54 Average	17.97	5.75
1955-64 Average	26.14	3.90
1965-74 Average	30.68	3.37
50-year Average	22.12	4.94
Year 1968	36.07	2.78
Year 1969	33.49	3.00
Year 1970	26.94	3.74
Year 1971	32.75	3.02
Year 1972	35.42	2.83
Year 1973	28.72	3.52
Year 1974	19.86	5.17
January 1975	17.76	5.63
August 1975	21.19	4.72
September 1975	20.92	4.78

	Yields on Common Stock	*Yields on Corporate Bonds*	*Stock Yields as Multiples of Bond Yields*
1907-1916	5.71	4.69	1.22
1917-1926	7.11	5.33	1.33
1927-1936	5.58	4.45	1.25
1937-1946	5.77	2.88	2.00
1947-1956	5.80	2.89	2.01
1957-1966	3.69	4.34	.85
1967-1976	3.62	7.39	.49
Year 1973	3.52	7.56	.47
Year 1974	5.17	8.25	.62
Year 1975	4.85	8.64	.56
Year 1976	4.18	8.36	.50
Jan. 1977	4.11	8.02	.51
Feb.	4.30	8.14	.53
Mar.	4.37	8.19	.53
Apr.	4.38	8.14	.54

STOCK AND BOND YIELDS

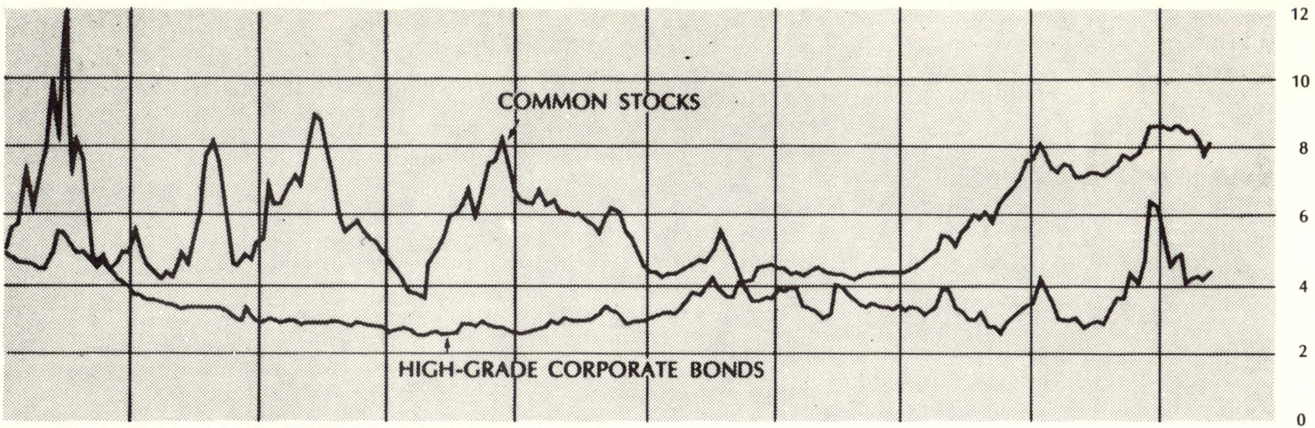

STOCK YIELDS AS MULTIPLES OF BOND YIELDS

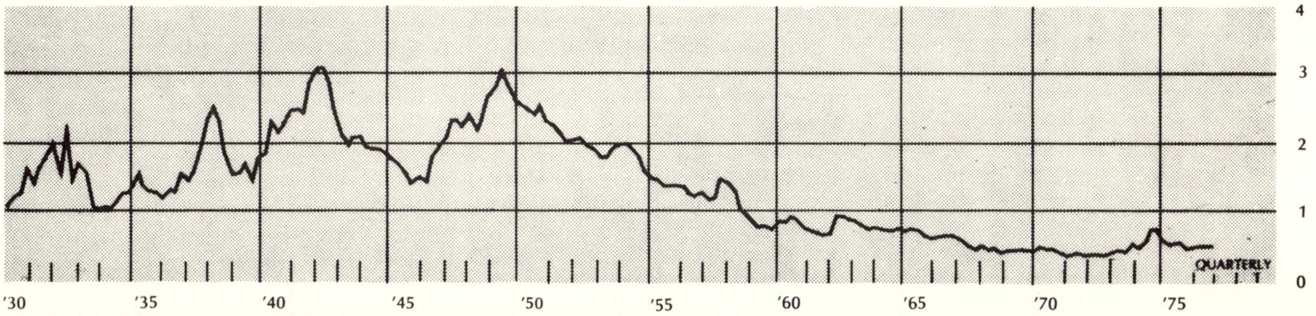

SOURCES: STANDARD AND POOR'S CORPORATION AND THE CLEVELAND TRUST COMPANY

There are many economic indicators that can be used to get an idea of the trend in the actual production of goods and services as opposed to money flows. I place special emphasis on capacity utilization ratios. Once production, especially in the basic industries, reaches 90% or better, further increases in output have to be met by expansion in capacity. However, construction of additional productive capacity usually takes a couple of years, but the decisions to expand are typically made when business is booming, profits are high, and enthusiasm rampant. The stock market, though, may have already reflected the bouyant business conditions and, therefore, signs of high-capacity utilization is a caution flag to the investor.

The best "check" on the money and sentiment indicators is the weekly or daily cumulative differential between advancing stocks and declining stocks. There is a fundamental and harmonious relationship between the DJIA and the A-D line. This normal relationship operates as follows: the two indicators tend to move together with the primary, secondary, and minor market trends. Furthermore, both indicators normally tend to confirm each other by penetrating preceding high or low points. Occasionally, there are important divergences between the DJIA and the A-D line. This is always considered abnormal action. A study of the relationship between these two indicators shows that when nonconformations appear, the result is an eventual reversal of the trend that produced the abnormality. Accordingly, the A-D line is useful in confirming the strength or weakness of the market itself. At the same time, the A-D line is useful in confirming the economic and psychological background. In other words, if you are in a bull market, the majority of stocks should be participating in the upswing. However, if the economic and corporate background is favorable, but the majority of stocks do not seem to be reacting to the good news, caution is indicated. Remember, the market is a discounting mechanism, while economic news is current history.

The chapter is not meant to be a lesson on how to use market indicators, but to introduce you to these valuable tools. A number of the books listed in chapter VIII, go into more detail on the use and construction of these tools and this is a good starting point. I tried to give you an idea of how indicators have been useful to me, but you must find out what strikes your fancy—what you like to rely upon—what aids you in making your critical decisions.

VII

TWENTY HELPFUL HINTS

The preceding pages have attempted to provide the initial steps for successful investing. Confidence and experience are the binding elements. Below are some helpful hints that should aid you in your investment program.

1. Play for big gains

Forget about the little ripples or the tempting trades. Concentrate your efforts on large potential moves in stock prices. Try to isolate trends where longevity is at least twelve months, preferably longer. These trends should be based upon solid foundations to ensure their durability. This is what produces winners providing profits of 100%, 200%, 300% over the years. By following this rule, in my opinion, you are likely to improve your chances for consistently making money.

2. Let your profits run

Don't close out your positions haphazardly. Just because a stock looks high temporarily, don't feel you *must* sell. If the story is still fresh and alive, continue to hold, particularly if the basic trend is still intact. Sell only when the future appears to be fully discounted or when the major underpinnings are beginning to change. This principle, combined with hint No. 1, increases the odds for amassing large amounts of capital.

3. Cut your losses short

When you think you have made a mistake, don't procrastinate. Sell! You're bound to make errors. Be objective, not emotional, and face up to losses quickly. Taking a loss can be an agonizing experience. It's very hard to admit you were wrong, but it will be your cheapest sale. Small losses have a habit of becoming large losses, creating serious problems. Concentrating on big gainers, letting your profits run, and cutting your losses short allow the power of compounding to work in your favor and increase probabilities of a high rate of return.

4. Periodically recheck your holdings

Don't buy 'em and put 'em away. Things do change. Managements grow old or complacent. The competitive situation can change. Patents can run out. New inventions or developments can have a profound effect upon an industry or company. The newfangled automobile in the 1920s had a major effect on the horse and buggy. The semiconductor had a devastating effect on the transistor producers. So don't buy and forget about your holdings.

5. When nervous, sell to your comfort zone

If something is bothering you about the market or a particular stock, don't be afraid to lighten up. When you get uneasy about something, it's usually a sign that you sense some trouble, but are unable to identify the specific source. Listen to your instincts, they're probably right! Continue to sell until you reach the point where you are no longer anxious. The comfort zone will differ with every individual. After all, owning stocks should be a pleasurable experience.

6. Forget about tips and inside information

There are no secrets in the stock market. Inside information and tips have only a transitory effect on prices. Moreover, tips rarely work out. They are usually based upon flimsy facts or "get-rich-quick" schemes. Remember, probably by the time you have heard the "tip" or special information, so have dozens of other people and it's already reflected in the price of the stock.

7. *Don't talk about your holdings to anyone*

Don't be casual about your holdings and discuss them with every Tom, Dick, and Harry. Your stocks are personal to you. You know why you bought them. You know what you are discounting. Others do not and they can undermine your opinion, create doubts in your mind, and shake your confidence—causing you to make a poor decision.

8. *You don't have to be in the market all the time*

Don't let your cash burn a hole in your pocket! Resist the temptation to always buy! buy! If you can't find a stock you really like, hold onto your money. Don't compromise just because stocks are going up. Stick to your principles, you'll do better in the long run. Don't always be a bull. Remember, markets go both up and down, and there are times to take profits and return to the sidelines.

9. *Don't try to buy at bottoms and sell at tops*

Nobody can be that precise. Stocks tend to go to extremes based upon either pessimism or optimism. Don't be a hero in a downtrend and guess at bottoms. Stocks have a way of disappointing the crowd and continuing to go even lower. Conversely, don't wait to sell at tops. That's the greed and smart aleck instinct, and the market rarely accommodates the pig or the arrogant.

10. *Don't look back over your shoulder*

It does little good to "cry over spilt milk." Cry babies rarely succeed. Learn from your experience and quickly move on. Be crisp and maintain a sense of humor. Recognize you will make mistakes—just cut them short. If you have a "I should have done this" or "I should have done that" attitude, it's likely to affect your next move. Be positive!

11. *Don't buy laggard stocks unless you have a good reason*

Stay with industry leaders. They usually are the most profitable, the industry price leaders, and the strongest companies. Accordingly, they usually set the pace for their industry. Investors recognize this and the shares receive the best support and sponsorship. Secondary stocks or securities that do not keep pace with the industry leaders should be avoided unless you have well-defined reasons for purchase.

12. Don't rely on projections and economic forecasts

Individual company projections and economic forecasts have their place in investment analysis. However, no one can predict the future with certainty and the typical batting average is not major league. Use your common sense and ask yourself, "Do the forecasts seem reasonable based upon my own observations?" Take long-term company projections that defy history or company experience or reasonable probabilities with a grain of salt. Overreliance on projections or forecasts can be costly.

13. If you change the reason why you purchased a stock, sell!

Let's face it! If you have to begin to come up with new reasons to explain why you bought your stock, you're probably rationalizing a mistake. Keep clear in your mind what you are discounting. If you have to change the reason for purchasing the stock, then something is not working out according to your expectations.

14. Typically, you get what you pay for

The market is efficient and most stocks are fairly priced at any given point in time. Fire sales occur only when pessimism is rampant. Quality wears well, like everything else. There is better ownership, better sponsorship, and, most importantly, a record of more earnings and dividends behind each share than so-called bargains.

15. Price is important

Simply stated, the price you pay ultimately determines the rate of return you earn. Distinguish between the company and its stock. The company may be doing very well but the stock may be exorbitantly priced. The company doesn't know you own it; you own the shares.

16. Don't average down unless you have a good reason

An initial decline is usually the beginning of a trend. Unless you can identify the reasons and are satisfied with the answers, don't average down. Cut your losses short. Bad news is usually followed by more bad news, and what seems like a bargain today, can be very expensive tomorrow.

17. The crowd is always wrong—not true!

This is one of the most dubious Wall Street adages. Most people assume the crowd is always wrong, but by definition, you cannot have a trend unless the majority of people agree. It's only at extremes, or critical turning points that it pays to cross the crowd. Contrariness for the sake of contrariness rarely pays. Remember, the crowd *is* usually right.

18. The market is always right in the final analysis

The market always has the last word. It doesn't know your opinion or hopes. It's impartial, totally objective, and cold-blooded. The market discounts the past, present, and future, all the known and unknown. Be humble! Remember what Tallyrand said, "There is somebody who knows more than anybody and that's everybody."

19. The news follows the trend

The news rarely creates or causes a trend; events not newspaper stories are the real factors. The news may condition the psychology, but the market reacts to real factors and is constantly discounting the future. The news is always bleak at the bottom and optimistic at the top. The market made a bottom in 1970 and headed upward when the papers sensationalized the Penn-Central bankruptcy. When the market shrugs off bad news, that's bullish; when it ignores good news, beware!

20. *Knowing how to capitalize on success and to curtail losses is more important than superior selection or superior timing*

Cutting losses and letting your profits run are basic to successful investing. However, none of us can consistently boast of superior selection or superior timing. Accordingly, the best road to profits lies in learning how to utilize your best thoughts and to minimize your worst. This takes understanding yourself and self-confidence.

VIII

START YOUR OWN LIBRARY

Having been exposed to the "essentials" for investing, you are now ready for further exploration. Successful investing is not different from any other field. It takes time, study, experience, and devotion. Leading lawyers or doctors continue to keep up with their professions through supplemental reading, journals, books, and refresher courses. It's no different in the market. So keep on studying and reading. Develop a library! You will be surprised how it opens up new vistas. You may be stimulated to think about new methods or better ways to do old things. You will be able to tap the minds and experience of many intelligent people and fashion their messages to your own experiences. You will be a better investor by making this effort. Below is a suggested bibliography for a starter library. Add to the list other works you find useful and interesting.

The Psychological Aspects of Markets:

Mackay, Charles. Extraordinary *Popular Delusions and the Madness of Crowds*. Boston, Massachusetts: L.C. Page and Company, 1932

Magee, John. *The General Semantics of Wall Street*. Lakeville, Connecticut: Institute of General Semantics, 1958

Seldon, G.C. *Psychology of the Stock Market*. Wells, Vermont: Fraser Publishing Company, 1965

Economics:

Keynes, John Meynard. *The General Theory of Employment, Interest and Money*. New York: Harcourt Brace Jovanovich, Inc., 1965

Samuelson, Paul A. *Economics*. New York: McGraw-Hill Book Co., 1976

Security Analysis:

Graham, Benjamin; Dodd, David L.; and Cottle, Sidney. *Security Analysis*. 4th ed. New York: Mcgraw-Hill, 1962

Charting and Technical Analysis:

Edwards, Robert and MaGee, John. *Technical Analysis of Stock Trends*. Springfield, Massachusetts: John MaGee, 1948

Granville, Joseph E. *A Strategy of Daily Stock Market Timing for Maximum Profit*. Englewood Cliffs, New Jersey: Parker Publishing Co., Prentice-Hall Inc., 1976

Neill, H.B. *The Art of Contrary Thinking*. Caldwell, Idaho: Caxton Printers Ltd., 1963

Of General Interest:

Baruch, Bernard. *My Own Story*. New York: Holt, Rinehart and Winston Inc., 1957

Galbraith, John Kenneth. *The Great Crash*. New York: Houghton Mifflin Co., 1972

Graham, Benjamin. *The Intelligent Investor*. New York: Harper and Row Pubs. Inc., 1973

Lefeure, Edwin. *Reminiscences of a Stock Operator*. Boston: Financial Publishing Co., 1976

Rosenberg, Claude N., Jr. *Stock Market Primer*. New York: Warner Books, Independent News Co., 1970

Schwed, Fred. *Where Are the Customers Yachts?* New York: Simon and Schuster, Inc., 1955

Smith, Adam. *The Money Game*. New York: Random House Inc., 1976

Sprinkel, Beryl Wayne. *Money and Stock Prices*. Homewood, Illinois: Richard D. Irwin, 1964

Modern Thought and Theory:

Brealey, Richard A. *An Introduction to Risk and Return from Common Stock.* Cambridge, Massachusetts: The M.I.T. Press, 1969

Cohen, Jerome B. and Edward D. *Investment Analysis and Portfolio Management.* Homewood, Illinois: Richard D. Irwin, 1967

Lorie, and Hamilton. *The Stock Market Theories and Evidence.* Homewood, Illinois: Dow-Jones Irwin Inc., 1973

Mendelson and Roberts. *Investment Analysis and Security Markets.* New York: Basic Books, Inc., 1976

Personal Investment Philosophy:

Fisher, Philip A. *Common Stocks and Uncommon Profits.* rev. ed. New York: Harper and Row, 1960

Loeb, G. M. *Battle for Investment Survival.* New York: Simon and Schuster, 1965

Rosenberg, Claude N. Jr. *The Common Sense Way to Stock Market Profits.* New York: New American Library, 1969

Bank Letters:

Quarterly Review. Federal Reserve Bank of New York

U.S. Financial Data. Federal Reserve Bank of St. Louis
Review. Federal Reserve Bank of St. Louis
Monthly Economic Letter. Citibank

Government Publications:

Business Conditions Digest. U.S. Government Printing Office
Survey of Current Business. U.S. Government Printing Office

IX

SOME RANDOM THOUGHTS

Wall Street never ceases to amaze me. It's a cross between Madison Avenue and Macy's, and seldom a place for real investment. When stocks are truly attractive for investment, everybody's bearish.

Invest with a sense of humor. Don't take yourself seriously, for in the long run, the market makes fools out of all of us.

Strategy is nothing but glorified trading.

Beware of the super-sophisticated approaches

and techniques for investing. They tend to outsmart the practitioners. Remember, there is considerable elegance in simplicity.

Random walk sounds like a new dance craze, while *beta* sounds like some kind of social disease.

Like every profession, Wall Street's jargon is designed to make the layman confused and the business sound complicated. The truth is, the business is simple. All you need to do is buy "low" and "sell" high.

I still haven't found out who "they" are. However, I hear about these mysterious people as if there was a special inner circle that is privy to everything.

Investors are their own worst enemies. Fear and greed predominate human emotions in the stock market.

Smart people are rarely money-makers on Wall Street, as they are too busy proving how smart they are. It's the shrewd ones who are the winners.

For most people, Wall Street is the world's greatest casino. The only trouble is you get dividends to remind you how stupid you were.

Analysts are like sheep. They bore you with known information and forget that money-making is discounting the future.

If analysts are like sheep, then the typical investor is like a lamb led to slaughter. He "beep, beeps" to the tape, to the newspaper, to forecasts, to authoritative accounts, to research reports, to brokers, to government doubletalk, etc., etc., etc.

The small investor can successfully compete with the institutional investor. The latter may have greater access to a mass of minutia, but no one has a corner on the interpretation or relevant trends. All it takes is devotion, hard work, knowledge, and judgment of facts already in the public domain and a flair for discounting the future.

Charting is like modern art—abstract and incomprehensible. You can see anything in the picture you want to.

As Lord Keynes wrote, the market is like a game of musical chairs, and you hope you're not caught standing when the music stops. However, too much time is spent trying to outguess the other players, and not enough time to look at the basic facts and trends.

The only trouble with indicators is that they must be interpreted.

For most players, the market is really a game of ego instead of a place to make money. That's too boring!

Research is putting together bits and pieces of information to solve a puzzle or problem. It entails a delicate art of interpretation and a sixth sense of when to act. Those who act too hastily assume greater risks, while those who wait for the puzzle to become clear, accept only nominal returns.

As the saying goes, "If you're so smart, why aren't you rich?" The answer I'd like to give is, "I am!" Instead of, "I'm still trying!"

If analysts are sheep, economists are the worst of the bunch. They're the only group that can explain why they were wrong and make you feel stupid in the process.

X

A POSTSCRIPT

A number of people who read this manuscript felt let down at the end. They all said something was missing. "How to do it?" As I mentioned in the preface this was not meant to be a text book, or a primer, or a how-to-do-it book. If there is any message worth remembering it is that there are no recipes for making money in the market. The key is to be flexible and adaptable. However, before you embark upon an investment program you should take the time to explore your inner psyche. Try to understand your motives, your strengths, your weaknesses. Free yourself from your prejudices, these are limitations that will impede your success. Set yourself some goals that are related to your capabilities and desires. The rest is hard work. That may sound boring or prosaic, but hours of thought and study do bring rewards. I know of no other way. Playing the market is not romantic, but a cold, hard-boiled business.

A Postscript

All of us are shaped by our experiences in life. Most of my comments were born of deep-rooted conviction and personal happenings. I think the events which occurred during the first years of my career in Wall Street made the deepest impressions on me and shaped my beliefs. Subsequent events have only served to reinforce these lessons.

Originally, I did not intend to work in Wall Street, but sought a job in the corporate world. I wanted to be a captain of industry! After many interviews and personal frustrations, I finally took stock of myself—relating my education, training, and abilities to my goals and personality. It became clear to me that I should be in the stock and bond business, so I headed downtown and was fortunate enough to land a job with a leading brokerage house. I was progressing well and felt the time had come for me to handle my family's securities business. Over the years my father's dealings were entrusted to a cagey old-timer, but his prodigal son was now a sixty-day wonder.

So with good intentions and a large sum of money my investment career really began. Knowing that I was still somewhat green, but cocksure of myself, I sought out a close friend who had been in the business a number of years to "guide" me along the way. Well, the result was a disaster. We went along with the arrangement for almost a year when I realized something was wrong. I took one look at what I owned, reflected on all the illusionary profits and stories I had been fed by my friends, and realized I was slowly being taken to the cleaners. I was panic stricken. My portfolio consisted of tertiary and secondary securities of dubious long-term values. Drastic action was called for. So, without hesitation, I ordered the entire portfolio sold immediately and I took my losses.

Now the real task was before me. I had to restore the faith my parents had placed in me and make back the large losses. Now I knew I could not expect anyone else to help me, but I was still relatively inexperienced. I attacked the problem with all the determination and furor at my command. But first I had to get the necessary knowledge to succeed. Luckily, the firm where I was employed had a first-rate library. I immersed myself in reading everything I could get my hands on. I read the literature of the 1920s; descriptions of stock markets going back to the 1790s in Europe; books on technical analysis, trading theories and techniques, and economic and monetary factors relating to stock markets; and literature pertaining to individual company backgrounds on every New York Stock Exchange listing. I must have covered about five years of work inside of a few weeks.

With better preparation, I reentered the market. Luckily for me, I recouped every penny lost, and then some, within three months. That experience taught me some valuable lessons that I have never forgotten. First, it would have been easier and less costly to learn with a small sum of money. Next, don't seek crutches. True success can come only from within you. Adequate preparation and knowledge are essential, then you must have the confidence to act upon your own convictions. Third, set realistic goals and then have the determination and aggressiveness to see them achieved. This may mean total absorption and concentration on what you are doing. Finally, have faith in your own ability, which will be reinforced through experience.

There were also many psychological traits I learned I had, such as my reactions to loss, stress, achievement, elation, fear, greed, frustration, joy, and impatience. Of course, I was able to put to test many of the trading techniques and stock market axioms I had read about. Most important of all, I was able to develop my style and manner of doing things that best suited my personality.

My personal story is only meant to illustrate the catalyst that brought most things together for me. I had an advantage in that my schooling and training was in economics and finance so that the time period of learning could be compressed. In addition, I seemed to have natural talent for finance and loved the work. However, I have known scores of people with majors in biology, English, anthropology, and so forth, who turned out to be very successful investors. You can also join their ranks.

First, you must develop some fundamental skills. A prerequisite is reading a financial statement. An elementary knowledge of accounting is helpful. Next an understanding of how business operates will make the numbers in a financial statement more meaningful. Some background of economics is also desirable since companies do not operate in a vacuum. After you have mastered these skills, you will be able to determine whether you have a feeling for numbers and have an analytical mind.

What I have outlined sounds formidable and time-consuming. However, it needn't be. Yes, you should do a lot of reading on your own. That's the purpose of the beginning reading list provided in chapter VIII. An easy way to get started on your education is to take a course on investments given by many colleges, adult education courses, night schools, and investment clubs. There you will learn the techniques of security analysis, the fundamentals of corporate finance, and the relationships between money and credit. Now you will be ready to experiment on your own with your own money. The real adventure will start!

GLOSSARY

ADVANCE-DECLINE LINE. The cumulative differential between the cumulative number of advancing stocks and the cumulative number of declining stocks. It is constructed as follows:

Daily Advances	*Daily Declines*	*Cumulative Advances*	*Cumulative Declines*	*Cumulative Differential*
800	400	800	400	400
1000	500	1800	900	900
600	400	2400	1300	1100
300	600	2700	1900	800

CAPACITY UTILIZATION RATIO. The percentage of current production to rated output at full production. For example, a steel mill could produce 100,000 tons daily at capacity, but if current production is only 80,000 tons daily it is said to be operating at 80% capacity.

CHARTIST. *See* TECHNICIAN.

CHARTS. The working tools of the technician. They can be developed in a multitude of forms and styles to graphically represent almost anything and everything that takes place in the market.

COMMON STOCK. Ordinary capital stock in a company without a definite stated dividend rate or the privilege of preferred stock, but usually gives the owner a vote at stockholders' meetings in proportion to his holdings.

COMPOUND INTEREST. Interest paid on both principal and the accumulated unpaid interest; to earn interest on interest.

DISCOUNT. In stock market terms, to act upon an event beforehand; to anticipate an event or happening.

DOW JONES INDUSTRIAL AVERAGE (DJIA). An index composed of thirty stocks weighted by market value of the capitalization of each company. The index is supposed to reflect the trend of the market either up or down.

EARNINGS LEVERAGE. The effects of rises and declines in a business-operating rate relative to its capacity and break-even levels. It is particularly evident in companies where plant investment is a large factor in costs compared to direct labor costs.

EQUITY. The interest of the stockholders in a company as measured by the capital and surplus.

EXCESS RESERVES. Member bank deposits with the Federal Reserve banks over and above the required legal minimum.

FREE RESERVES. The total excess reserves minus member bank indebtedness to the Reserve banks, or net excess reserves.

HEDGE FUND. A form or organization for the management of money whereby the manager may be long a portion of his portfolio and short another portion in order to balance his risk. Hedge funds usually are not registered with the Security and Exchange Commission and take the form of partnerships.

LEVERAGE. The condition which causes wide swings in per share earnings and market value, arising because a company's common stock has relatively heavy fixed costs or deductions (interest and/or preferred dividends). Small changes in operating revenues or operating can have a magnified change on per share earnings.

MONEY SUPPLY. Currency in circulation, demand deposits, and net time deposits, other than negotiable time certificates of deposit issued in denominations of $100,000 or more by large weekly reporting commercial banks.

MULTIPLE. *See* PRICE/EARNINGS RATIO.

ODD-LOT. The purchase or sale of less than one hundred shares of stock. One hundred shares or multiples of a hundred are called round lots.

ODD-LOT SHORT INTEREST. The number of shares sold short by less than round-lot sales.

PRICE/EARNINGS RATIO (P/E). Market price divided by the current annual earnings per share. Example: Stock selling for 100 and earning $10 per share has a price earnings ratio of 10 to 1, or is said to be selling at ten times earnings.

SHORT INTEREST. The amount of shares sold short as reported monthly by the New York and American exchanges. A short arises from the sale of stock not already owned, in anticipation of a decline in price.

SHORT INTEREST RATIO. The monthly reported short interest divided by the average daily volume for the particular month. For instance, if the short interest is 15,000,000 shares and the daily average volume is 15,000,000 shares, then the short interest ratio is 1.

STANDARD AND POOR'S 425 INDEX. An index composed of 425 industrial companies weighted by market value of the capitalization of each company. The index is supposed to reflect the trend of the market. Since it is a broader index than the DJIA, many investors feel it is more representative of the underlying trend than that in the Dow.

STANDARD AND POOR'S 500 INDEX. The same index as the S & P 425 except it includes utility stocks and, therefore, is broader.

TECHNICAL ANALYSIS. The study of the action of the market itself. It involves the art of recording, usually in graphic form, the actual history of trading, such as price changes, volume of transactions, and short interest, in a certain stock or in the "averages" and determining from that pictured history the probable future trend.

TECHNICIAN. One who studies and uses technical analysis to determine the future direction of a given stock or market.

YIELD. The return on an investment expressed as a percentage of cost. It is found by dividing the market price into the dividend rate for stocks. Example: Stock selling for 100 and paying a dividend of five dollars is said to yield 5%.